BEAUTY FOR ASHES

CONSPIRACY, BETRAYAL, & REDEMPTION

The Jocelyn Ja'Net Story

JOCELYN J. WILLIS

Foreword by Bishop Richard E. Young

BEAUTY FOR ASHES

CONSPIRACY, BETRAYAL, & REDEMPTION

The Jocelyn Ja'Net Story

Contents

In loving memory of
Brandon Scott Johnson
1981-2015

Dedication

In my lifetime I've discovered a multitude of individuals who are shackled by silence. I salute you for your bravery as you embark upon this journey. It's with deep gratitude that I applaud you for stepping beyond fear. I dedicate this book to my younger self, that awkward long lanky kid with glasses. I tribute this book to you, for going beyond the crushing period called, "I'm not smart enough," this is for you. You hurdled over the devastation that tried to erase your existence and for that, I am tremendously proud of you!

Foreword

Seldom does a pastor speak on behalf of a member of his congregation, he esteems to be extraordinary in character and talent. Jocelyn is exactly that, extraordinary, and talented. I've witnessed her growth under my leadership for twenty-one years. At the age of nineteen-years-old, Jocelyn shared something personal with me about her life story. I recall sharing with Jocelyn that God was going to heal her from her devastating past.

This prolific writer has experienced a great deal in life, enabling her to pen with accuracy of purpose. Each line in Beauty for Ashes is filled with intent of purpose, exposing Jocelyn Willis' personal pains and joys, while portraying vivid pictures in our mind.

I believe that Jocelyn has transferred much of her belief and life experiences to these pages. In her unique and soft way, she helps us go on a journey of self-revelation. She guides us with the most powerful weapon known to man, "The Word of God" and the zeal of her intellect.

My continuous prayer is that everyone is restored to the joy of their salvation despite your past and your pain.

I'm very proud of you, daughter, and as always, "I expect great things from you!"

Bishop Richard E. Young
Pastor Emeritus
The Chosen Vessel Cathedral
Fort Worth, Texas 76119

Introduction

With my heart lavishing in immeasurable honor, I am honored to prepare you for a life changing experience. Before you begin this journey with me through my timeline, I pray one thing, and that's FREEDOM. Whatever has you shackled in captivity, I command it to leave during the tenure of reading this book. The writings within these very pages weren't created to entertain you, but to transform you. I was enjoined to give birth to what you are holding in your hands. God called me to a place of submission unto Him. It is with great privilege to submit to the will and purpose of God. Before I began this process of reflection, I really didn't know where to start. God said that He was going to bring things to my remembrance on how to write the book. I was intrigued by His request. In this season of my life, I wasn't serious about my writing, nor was I ready to write about my life. When God summons you to do something, however, you must do it. After all, God will never lead you wrong. I had followed many pathways in life but one thing I do know is that He has never led me down a devastating pathway. I battled many things, by going left when He wanted me to go right. Those decisions caused me to suffer massive consequences. After experiencing a fiery hell right here on earth and making it out, I had to speak about it. GOD was speaking to my spirit saying, "My daughter, it's time!"

My prayer for you TODAY, is that my story will be a reminder that God can do the same for you! I decided to accept God's request of writing this book, and by doing so I decided to stand upon my

STORY, and not in it! You are divinely called to confront things that hold you captive, whether it be fear, doubt, hurt or despair. I command strongholds to be destroyed with the turning of each page, while God holistically sets you FREE!

Behold, at that time
I will deal with all who afflict you;
I will save the lame,
And gather those who were driven out;
I will appoint them for praise and fame
In every land where they were put to shame.
At that time I will bring you back
Even at the time I gather you;
For I will give you fame and praise
Among all peoples of the earth,
When I return your captives
before your eyes,"
Says the Lord.

Zephaniah 3:19-20 NKJV

"And they overcame him by the blood of the Lamb, and by the word of their testimony, and they did not love their lives to the death.

Revelations 12:11

CHAPTER 1

Earth Light

A great manifestation surfaced beyond obstruction.

I f I could recall my earliest memory, it would be the tender age of five years old. I lived in a huge neighborhood near tall buildings and fields of grass where kids would play football. The sidewalks were miles long and I'd find myself speeding swiftly down them on my Big Wheel, which I imagined was propelled by a powerful race car engine. It never appeared to me that my life was impoverished and that my family and I needed all the help we could get. My five-year-old perspective was captivated by sitting on the porch eating ice cream. My mother clearly couldn't afford the yummy sweet goodness. But Mama made ways for my brother and I growing up as small children in Fort Worth, Texas. God somehow sent angels to provide for us when our mama couldn't. I remember this little lady who lived a few doors down from me and her name was Ms.

Callie. She was a tiny little thing, very small in stature, but her heart sure was big! She became my POPSICLE SAVIOR! The tinkling of the bells would ring so loudly as the ice cream man drove down our street. My little legs would run as fast as they could take me. I'd scream at the top of my lungs inside our house that was really a two bedroom apartment. Inside our home, my big brother and I shared a room. "Mama, oh Mama," I'd shout, "I need twenty-five cents for an ice cream!" You know what, I never got that quarter from my mother. I'd run over to Ms. Callie's house and she'd answer the door as her granddaughter Latrice stood by her. We called her Trice for short. Ms. Callie would reach into her pocket and hand Trice and I a quarter. We'd run fast as we could to the tuck to get our popsicle.

Do you remember the red, white and blue ones that looked like a rocket? Those were the best. Trice and I headed back to her granny's porch to enjoy our sweet treat. She and I were like peas and carrots; we were best friends, I truly adored her. Latrice was something special, she and I would play together nearly each day if it was up to us. She was so short, and I had these long lanky legs, but we were both thin. Come to think of it, I towered over her in height. When we met, we became instant friends. She was my everything, next to my big brother of course. I'd share all my secrets with her, ninety-nine percent of them she never could keep. When the streetlights came on, we'd say our good-byes and go home.

My mama worked very long hours, which left my brother Chris in the kitchen cooking our meals. He became the authority figure when Mama would have to go to work. I'd come into the house and I'd hear music blasting from our old school radio. He would sing at the top of his lungs, belting out, "Get down on it, come on and get down on it." The kitchen would smell like the usual, fried chicken and beans. My brother didn't have a choice, he had to cook, or we would starve. I don't think he minded cooking, considering the way he would dance around the kitchen. Flour would be everywhere, and the kitchen was a hot mess. He tried his best, and I was just happy to have dinner on the table. As we'd sit down to eat, I would hear the loudest sound coming from the kitchen window.

MAMA PICTURED HERE IN 1972

Mama would walk in exhausted, trying not to let us know how truly tired she really was. She worked extremely hard. I knew exactly who she got her work ethic from, and that was my grandmother. Mama was nicknamed "Buttons" as a kid, because she had a round face and the chubbiest cheeks. She had the prettiest smile and was shaped like a Coke bottle. I never understood why I was so small while my mother was built like a brick house. If Mama wasn't working, she made constant trips to the doctor's office. I heard stories about my mama having babies before I was born. I was informed that she lost three of them, two of which were a set of

3

twins. Growing up, I wished the babies would have lived, especially the baby boy. My brother Christopher truly wanted a brother and he demonstrated that desire on poor little old me. My brother was the oldest and our mother named him Christopher Michael Willis, but I call him, Brother.

CHRIS & JOCELYN IN 1985-1986

GRANDMA MAURICE WILLIS   GRANDPA VAWYER WILLIS

He was my king in the house and I'd always follow him around. We were Big Frank and Maurice's grandchildren, and they lived in Munday, Texas. Munday was a small country town in West Texas. Many people called our grandfather Big Frank, but his name was Vawyer Willis. He was a big man and he had huge hands. I never got the opportunity to meet him. My grandfather passed away before I was born. I've only heard stories about him and seen a few pictures of him. I recall his children mentioning his bad temperament. Mama told me that she heard cries from my grandmother when she was a young person. She believed her mom was getting physically abused by her father. It was very heartbreaking to hear this, and that it could have happened in our bloodline. Sadly, my brother and I shared in our grandfather's temperament.

Brother also has huge hands like our grandpa. Brother decided to use his hands doing what he loved and that was playing football. He also had a love for making up creepy imaginary monsters, one of them he named, *The Green Thang*. At one point, I thought it was because he loved anything green. He loved things like Army men, the Incredible Hulk and G.I. Joe. My brother would wait until Mama would turn off all the lights, so she could enjoy her favorite TV show. He would wait until she'd ask me to go and grab her a pillow from her bedroom. As I reached the corner of the hallway, he'd scare the living crap out of me, screaming out, "The Green Thang!" I'd trip and bump my head and guess where we were going... off to the emergency room.

Mama wanted to beat him silly with a belt, but you know, she never did. Our mama really wasn't a disciplinarian. She was the only parent in our home, and she did what she could to make ends meet. I would sometimes eavesdrop as she talked on the telephone.

I didn't let her catch me though. One day she was talking on the phone while she was holding a handful of envelopes. She was holding some bills trying to figure out which one she would pay. I hid behind the couch as she was talking loudly on the phone, and I heard her asking someone on the other end for some help with her bills. Then my mama began to cry. She would look at me and wipe her tears and ask me to bring her a cup of water and a hairbrush. Mama would call me into the living room, and I'd sit on the floor in between her legs as she combed my hair. She had huge hands that were so heavy. I would wiggle and scream because it felt like my scalp was on fire. Mama would say, "Girl, you are so tender headed." I never understood what she meant by that. I felt the pain of getting my hair combed. She'd go on to tell me, "You have all this hair and you got it from your daddy." My hair was so thick and wavy, so all my mama had to do was put water and hair grease on it. Mama called the texture of my hair "water wave hair". My hair would curl up and shrink as she dipped her brush in the water and applied the hair grease. She styled my hair with two ponytails, which had become my signature style. I had an outfit that I put together that went perfect with my two ponytails. I simply loved my pink ruffled dress, and accented it with my strawberry shortcake socks, all the way up to my knees.

Mama drove the daycare van and I loved riding with the kids on her route. It was a pleasure going to the daycare, but for some reason, I would get into so much trouble. I think Brother's energy was rubbing off on me. I stayed busy each day and my curiosity would run wild. One morning my vibration was soaring extremely high. My mom finished her route and we made it to the daycare. I stepped off the van, carrying my plastic bag of canned goods. The center was having a canned food drive for the needy and I wanted to lend a hand. I was about to turn four, and I loved helping others. I went inside the classroom and all the children were playing on the floor. I walked over to them and for some strange reason, I began to swing the bag of canned food in the air. I heard a loud thump and I looked down to see what it was. A little girl was laying on the floor with blood trickling down her forehead. The teachers asked what happened, and all the children pointed at me. I began shaking my head as they all cried out in harmony, "she did it!"

I was telling a huge lie because I was so afraid. As the tears began to run down my face, I was fearful of what was going to happen to me. I wasn't concerned about the injured kid on the floor, because I didn't realize the severity of the little girl's injury. Mama was so furious with me and she had to find a way to cover the injured child's medical bills. Surprisingly enough, I wasn't kicked out of the center and the little girl recovered. Hey, I never said I was a saint!

After school, evenings were chill at my house. My weekends were cool too. I remember this tall, dark-skinned man who would stop by periodically. He would stop in and stay for a brief period and then he'd leave. He'd say a quick hello to me and make his way to see my mother. I later realized that the man who made frequent stops to our home was my biological father. I was a young person, but I knew there was something not right about his visits. My mother didn't talk about him often, but she shared many conversations with him. I'd hear her ask him for financial support. I think she got fed up asking for help because she tried to get child support. He later told me that my mother threw the book at him. My mother was a hard worker and I knew she deserved help with taking care of me. After all, she wasn't alone when she created me, so I felt it was only right.

Some nights I'd stay up late watching television with my brother. We spent a lot of time together, and come to think of it, his dad wasn't present in his life either. We both saw my birth father in passing, as he would hand me a dollar bill. I was only five or six at the time when I saw him. I remember my mom talking with her cousin Lawanda about the two cousins they both were dating. That's right, my mom and my older cousin were dating these two popular cousins. Let's just say *Papa was a rolling stone*! I found out that my conception was significant. My father was married when he was seeing my mother. Mama said that he told her he was single when they first met. Now I know that was a big bold face lie from the pits of hell.

Mama and my cousin Lawanda both conceived babies with these two Tollie cousins. My cousin Gralin was born before me and we grew up playing together as kids. God was trying to prove something to the world when I was born. My cousin Lawanda decided to give her son the Tollie last name. I was so happy that my mother didn't go that route. I was proud to be a Willis. After all, it was my grandpa's name and it made me proud to carry his name. My mother gave me an additional middle name, after my birth father, but I excluded that name. I couldn't see myself carrying a name that wasn't full of light. I was elated to hear my teacher call my name during roll call. Jocelyn Willis. I'd smile right away.

As I grew older, I learned that my mother conceived another baby by my birth father, but the baby didn't make it. In fact, my mama had her fair share of losing and burying babies. She later lost a set of twins. After she went through something so traumatic, I'm so surprised that she would still want to conceive another baby. I'm guessing God had other plans, because I was born two months early weighing only two pounds. When I think about it, as an adult, I've always hated the summer heat. My mother gave birth to me in the month of March. I was ready to make my debut during springtime! I was destined to be here because I fought my way to gain weight as I would rest in the glass incubator. As I continued to develop, my weight increased.

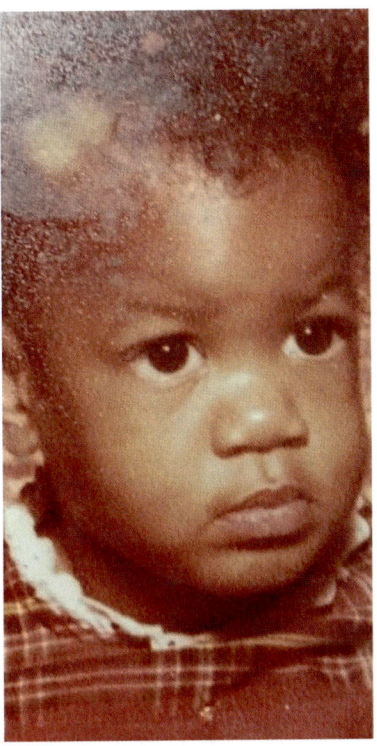

JOCELYN JA'NET WILLIS

She was unaware of the destiny that was before her!

Mama made frequent trips to the hospital to see her miracle baby. My mother never knew what was destined for her little baby girl. As she pondered the demise of her other babies, she watched me helplessly inside of the incubator. I can only imagine what could have been crossing her mind in that moment.

After a few weeks, I arrived home. Mama had family who would come and care for me. There were a few who had a hand in raising and caring for little Jocelyn. I was a blessed child, despite not having my biological father around. Most of my early years were spent on the Southside of Fort Worth, Texas. On a few occasions, Mama shipped us off to Decatur, Texas, to spend time with my cousins. I'd stay at a huge house that had railroad tracks right behind it, and lots of bedrooms inside. The front yard was filled with rocks and dirt and sticker bugs that would stick to my socks when I played outside. I enjoyed moments of eating watermelon on the front porch with my cousins. Those were the good old days, no worries and no problems. Now when I think of it, I never heard an ice cream truck out in the country, but that didn't bother me at all. Brother and I received so much love from our cousins, they were so happy to see us. My twice kin, Gralin Tollie lived out there as well and it was always great seeing him. We never hung out together with our fathers, but we did with our mothers' family. My great aunt Laura Johnson was the matriarch who cared for us all. I could never pronounce her name, so I called her Aunt Lena. I truly adored her; she was a sweet lady who would invite the masses over to her home.

She was very loving and hardworking, she treated us as if we were her very own children. Aunt Lena would wear her house dress and I loved seeing her walk in her bare feet around the house. She was some kind of wonderful! I cherished playing with my cousins outside. A sweet but stern voice would yell, "Children, it's time to come in for twelve o'clock prayer." I didn't want to stop playing just to come in and get on my knees to pray. I would do exactly as she asked, because if I was disobedient, I would feel a long switch on my backside. It was really a small thin branch from a tree. My cousins, brother and I would have to get down on our knees in front of the couch to pray. I never understood why she was so serious about praying. It wasn't until I began my relationship with the Lord that I discovered her reasoning for encouraging us to be consistent in prayer.

It felt like everyone in Decatur had a hand in raising me. I loved eating Honeycomb cereal in the morning after waking up from my cozy little pallet. We made little sleeping places on the floor using blankets and sheets because there were so many people sleeping over. We had epic sleepovers and every room was filled, including the living room floor. My Aunt Lena would assign a place for us to sleep. When nighttime would fall, we'd all lay out on the floor having the best conversations.

My Aunt Lena was raising eight children that she conceived with my great uncle Jimmy Neff Johnson. He was the brother of my grandmother. I didn't see him much, all I remember was lavishing in the arms of my dear Aunt Lena. There were times during my visits as a baby where my aunt and big cousins would encourage me to walk. I was having trouble learning to walk as a toddler, having experienced all sorts of medical issues. My Aunt Lena would reach her arms out to me saying, "Auntie Lena got you, baby girl." I'd place one foot in front of the other and tumble right on my bottom.

Surprisingly, even at a really young age, I was determined to succeed. The cheers were getting louder, and my little feet began taking off, and before I knew it, I was walking. The simple things in life meant so much to us as kids. We didn't have any worries, and each new day had a greater significance than the one before it. We never felt the weight our parents carried. One of my fondest memories is laughing and playing with my friends. Most mornings, my brother played the parent role by getting me ready for school.

Our mother had to be up early for work, which left my brother the responsibility of caring for me.

My first experience at public school was at Carol Leak Elementary. I was going off to kindergarten and I was so scared. I met my teacher; her name was Ms. Jackson. She wore a long green dress that hung down to her knees. Her legs were so long! I wonder if it was because of the high heels that she wore.

I became really well acquainted with Ms. Jackson, or should I say, with her measuring ruler. When the kids in her class would misbehave, she'd pop us on our hand as we stood on one foot. I never told my mother how she would discipline us.

I noticed at an early age, that I had trouble learning in class. Ms. Jackson would call me up to the number chart to count the numbers. When I heard my name called, "Jocelyn, please come up to the chart," I remember my eyes tearing up. I simply hated being in front of the class, my body felt weak and my heart would pound. I'd opened my mouth and I would count, saying the numbers aloud. The class would stare as if they were waiting for me to fail. Laughter would fill the room and my little heart was crushed. I was later sent to the nurse's office and on this visit, the nurse looked very concerned. I was sent back to class with a note.

The end of the school day had finally come. I couldn't wait to find out about the paper that was hanging from my shirt. Ms. Jackson stapled a note to the back my shirt. When I got home, Mama opened the letter and her face had the strangest look on it. I asked her about the note. Mama told me that she was taking me to John Peter Smith Hospital for a checkup. I didn't think much of it, so I took off running to see what my brother was doing in our room. I busted in the door screaming, "BROTHER!" and there he was, playing with his army men. I hated those things; he'd have thousands of them set up on the floor. It looked as if they were getting ready for battle. He would leave a few out after playing just so I could step on them. I'd scream to the top of my lungs as I held my aching feet.

The next day came like nightfall didn't exist. Mama was up getting dressed and I was trying to hurry and sneak my soiled sheets in the hamper. Mama would have been upset if she knew I had an accident while I was sleeping. Yes, I wet the bed from time to time. I'd climb into my brother's bed and sleep with him. I would try to hide my sheets, but I would always get caught. I would flip my mattress and end up getting stuck in between them. "Jocelyn Ja'Net, what are you doing?" Mama would call me to get out from beneath the mattresses. "Lord Jesus, what am I going to do with you?"

My little legs would take off, heading to the bathroom to take a bath. "You better be at this car by the time I'm ready to go!" Mama would shout. I quickly finished up and hopped in the car and we made it up to Main Street where the hospital was located. The hospital was huge, there was this monitor that would show the numbers. We'd take a ticket and wait to be called. I remember there were so many people in one room, all you could hear was coughing and sneezing. There were people holding babies and I saw plenty of mad faces. Number sixty-two was called and Mama and I walked back to a room with a long table. The doctor entered and asked me to put on a gown. He later put stickers and wires all over my chest. I had to lay on the table and try my best not to move. The doctors put cold jelly on my chest and took pictures of my heart.

After our visit to the doctor, Mama wasn't happy about the news she'd received. She explained to me that I had a hole in my heart. As I grew older, I learned that meant certain restrictions for me. I had big dreams of becoming a gymnast and I wanted to play basketball and run track. I was diagnosed with a heart condition called mitral valve prolapse, which consists of a heart murmur. The doctors said that there was a possibility that the hole in my heart would close. Nevertheless, I was crushed when I learned that I couldn't play sports. I had to get my heart checked from time to time. I didn't mind going to those appointments, because I would get to take a picture home of my heart. And I enjoyed the parties they would have for all the kids at the hospital.

Around this time, my life was consumed by multiple doctor's appointments. I'm sure that it was a trying time for my mother. She was a hero when it came to taking care of her children. The next day at school I would have my very own show and tell with my friends. During recess, I'd notice how hard I would breathe after jumping rope. My heart would beat funny even if I wasn't doing anything strenuous. My childhood was taking a downward spiral and my visits to the doctor increased. My mama was getting stressed as things progressed. She took me to get my spine checked out. There was a chance that I could possibly have a form of scoliosis. I hated seeing my mother miss work to take me to all my doctor's appointments. I was wondering, where was this God that she prayed to during these times? I sure didn't see Him helping us out, but maybe in some way He was there.

My mama was such an interesting lady, no matter how much she loved God, she made time for other things. She loved to spend time at the bingo hall where she would play cards for money. My mother loves to gamble, and I really think her first love was playing bingo. When she grabbed her purple bag, I knew exactly where she was going. When she returned home, she always brought something back with her. She smelled like cigarettes, while holding money in her hand. My brother and I didn't care too much, because we knew we would eat good that night. My mother would go to so many bingo sessions, that I was given the name *Bingo*. That nickname stuck with me until I was an adult. I dropped that name as I got older. On occasion I heard that name was birthed because my mother played her life away playing bingo. My family would say that when she was pregnant with me, she'd go and play from sun up to sun down. My uncle was the one who decided upon giving me that name. I was called all sorts of nicknames throughout the years. I later decided to stick with Jocelyn Ja'Net. I truly loved my name and I was very proud of it. I was named after an actress from the television series *Good Times*. My mama named me after Willona Woods, I loved her character on the show. Mama loved her name so much that she gave me her real birth name which was Ja'Net. Ja'Net Dubois is a classy lady with so much style. It's so ironic how her character is much of my personality to this very day.

As months went by, I returned to the hospital to get tested to see if I had Marfan Syndrome. The doctors would say that my legs and chest resembled a person with the syndrome. All the trips to the hospital were becoming tiresome. I would attend school and didn't want to play or pay attention in class. The days were excruciating for me and I was a bit distraught. After school I would lay around the house and watch television nonstop. I would sit so close to the television just to enjoy my favorite shows. I would lay comfortably while sucking my thumb as I watched that glowing, mesmerizing screen. It wasn't until my cousin put black pepper on it at night and the thumb sucking ended there.

Meanwhile, Mama noticed that I was squinting my eyes and she took me to get an eye exam. If I wasn't running into things, I was falling all over the place. This was the beginning of my roller coaster ride with the devil himself. I endured many hard days as a young person growing up. During those times I knew who could always cheer me up and that was my big brother. He always had a way of making things much better. I loved him a great measure, despite the fact that I had become a human target to him. I always thought of him when Mama and I would stop to get McDonald's for dinner. I'd always say, "Mama, don't forget about Brother," and she'd reply, "You are always thinking about Michael." She'd sometimes call him by his middle name. I'd smile and say, "Yes, I do!" He was a great brother, always looking out for Mama and me. He was the best brother ever.

Beloved, do not believe every spirit, but test the spirits, whether they are of God; because many false prophets have gone out into the world.

1 John 4:1

CHAPTER 2

Captivating Deception

A lie can appear in the form of flesh.

The summer was drawing near, and my brother and I discovered ways to have fun. If he wasn't playing football, he was trying to dodge me. I wanted to go everywhere he went. It was funny how he would try to sneak out of the house to go hang with his friends, Little Man and Montreal. He was fast, but I was much smarter! Chris would head straight for the front door, trying to creep past me without me knowing. Out of nowhere, you heard my loud but squeaky voice shouting, "BROTHER, where are you going!" I was adamant about spending time with my big brother. On a good day, I'd give him the saddest look I could muster up and yes, he'd give in. I always got my way, and out the front door we went to go play.

My brother was a cool kid, very popular in the Park Terrace Apartments. He went to Morning Side Middle School on the South

Side of Fort Worth. He had dreams of becoming a professional football player. He would have reached that dream too; the boy was cold on the field.

OUR HOME IN 1985 IN FORT WORTH, TEXAS

I couldn't wait to follow in his footsteps. I was hoping to attend Morning Side Middle School. You know, we were good kids, we never got into any trouble. Our days were simple, or at least to me they were. Mama worked nonstop; she'd leave early in the morning and come home late in the evening. The early memories of my mama were kind of bleak. I think maybe it was because she was the only bread winner in our home. The times when Mama made it home, I would be so thrilled. I loved spending time with her, especially when we would be snuggled up on the sofa.

My brother and I witnessed a hard-working provider in our in our home. I truly believe our mama learned her work ethic from my grandparents. My grandparents lived in a little country town, the dusty dirt roads of Munday, Texas. It was so small, it seemed as if everyone knew each other. My grandmother was Maurice Johnson and her husband was my grandfather, Vawyer Willis. The locals called him Big Frank; I'm thinking because he was a big man. He made a living as a farmer. He spent his days plowing cotton and gathering vegetables. Grandpa was a lover of denim overalls; I saw him wearing them in just about every photo. My grandparents raised three daughters together. My Aunt Gloria was their first born and second came my mother Joyce, and finally the baby girl Marva. These three were so foxy or at least I thought so.

My family and I would take these long road trips to Munday, it was way out west. When I got word that we were going out of town, I nearly flipped out. I was happier than Mama winning money at a game of bingo. "We are going to see Grandma!" I'd shout across the room. Upon our arrival, I always knew when we were getting close because I'd see the gas station called, Allsup's. Down the road was a Dairy Queen restaurant and we'd stop for ice cream Blizzards. The ice cream was the creamiest, and you could get any toppings your heart desired. I would always get an Oreo Blizzard and watch the cashier turn my cup upside down. It was like magic; the ice cream would never come out of the cup. My little legs would start swinging as I ate my icy cold treat.

From there it was a hop, skip and a jump to Grandma's house. We'd pull up to the cutest little pink house with a wooden fence with cats in the front yard. My grandma would greet us as she walked through the yard. She was small in stature, but although she was tiny, she was powerful. Ms. Maurice wasn't afraid of anything and I think living in Munday had something to do with it. She was sassy and adored red lipstick. She had a beautiful smile, and a gold tooth that sparkled. If you knew her, she would treat you like her very own child. My dear granny loved dressing up and wearing her wigs. The aroma wafting over from her kitchen always brought a big smile to my face. When we walked into her kitchen, she would have food already on the stove. We would all gather in the dining area for lunch. My grandma's hands were truly gifted. After a nice meal, we would hop in her car and she would show us around town. She loved to brag about her grandchildren. I loved her so much and she made sure I knew she loved me. After our tour of Munday, we would drive back to her house. My cousins and I would argue over who would sleep in the living room. No one wanted to sleep in the back rooms. I never worried about sleeping in those rooms, because I would sleep with Grandma.

Those bedrooms were kind of creepy to us. It was spooky and the floors made sounds when we'd walked to the back room. Inside there were pictures of us as babies near the beds sitting in frames. Looking at the pictures felt like a real-life picture album coming to life. My little five-year-old self would flop down in the bed and stare at my baby pictures. Grandma also had a huge Bible on her coffee table and her cooler unit blew some of the coldest air on earth. I could chill a glass of water sitting right in her living room. My grandma loved the Lord, but she'd curse like a sailor. Honey child, she would curse you in a quick minute!

During our visits, we'd sit down with her to enjoy tasty meals she prepared in her hot kitchen. My grandma was known for her home cooking. You could smell the aroma in the air as it soared through the screen door. She made fried chicken, okra, hush puppies and peach cobbler. After squeezing in her small dining area to eat, she'd put a plate on the stove. My grandma was very kind, and she loved feeding people. She would save a plate for this neighborhood guy named Kookum. I'm not sure if that was his real name or not.

She made a living working for a wealthy Caucasian lady. My grandma didn't have a fancy job, she worked as a housekeeper and boy was she good at it. No matter where she went, she was admired by the town people of Munday, Texas. I recall a few people mentioning how pretty Ms. Maurice was and how nice she dressed. Honey, let me tell you, my grandma loved to dress. She was the definition of a fashionista. Even if she didn't have anything to do or anywhere to go, she would dress up. One afternoon I asked her if she had any plans because she was so dolled up. She had her signature styled lipstick on, and she looked gorgeous. My grandma replied, "You never know, I may have a date." I'd smile while laughing at her hilarious sense of humor. I would lay in her bed staring at her as she put on her clip-on earrings. She would make huge circles of rouge blush on her cheeks. Lastly, she would apply her red lipstick, I couldn't wait until I could wear lipstick. She'd turn around and say, "Bingo, if you brush Grandma's wig, I'll give you a butterscotch." I'd say yes, and little did she know, I would have done it for free. She was my real-life candy girl. "Bingo," she'd say, "do you want to ride with me to Allsup's? Grandma needs some chewing gum and green alcohol." Before I could even say yes, she had her purse and was headed out the door. We'd zoom down the dusty dirt roads as if the police were after us. I jumped out of the car making sure my pennies were safe in my pocket. I knew exactly where I was going and that was to the penny candy section. "Alright, Bingo, let's go," and we walked to the car. She would slide me a piece of her green chewing gum. My granny and I would chew our gum like some cute divas on a road trip. Those are some of the fondest memories I recall of the precious time that I shared with my lovely grandmother.

Nightfall in the country was totally different than in the city. My family and I would panic because we were afraid of the fire ants and scorpions and just about any insects. One night, as my brother was preparing for bed, he let out a loud scream. I didn't know what was wrong, but he was terrified. My grandmother came running to see what was wrong. He yelled out that something had bitten him, and she told us that we all are scary as hell. She followed up with examining his hand. He got bit on his thumb after he noticed the scorpion was in his underwear. My grandma put tobacco in her mouth and removed the stinger. She followed with the green rubbing alcohol. My grandma wasn't scared of anything. She turned to look at our distraught little faces. "I tell you; you all are scared of any old thing!" But of course, she cursed. After I saw the fear on my brother's face, I was ready to go back to Fort Worth. I didn't want anything biting me.

The next morning, I was awakened to the smell of bacon frying and coffee brewing. I bet my grandma woke up with the roosters. She was dressed and we had to get up and get our day started. Grandma made sure we had a full stomach heading back home. She'd even send us off with some brownies. I hated saying goodbye to my grandma, it was awful. She would walk us out to the car and made sure she gave us the biggest hug. I would always stare out of the back window as we drove away.

You could see the dust in the air as Grandma stood waving goodbye. As she faded into the background, I would miss her even in that moment. The ride home to Fort Worth was such a long drive, but I didn't really care too much. I'd open my eyes and we were parked in front of our apartment, 2452 Elizabeth Court. I was so happy to be home and I couldn't wait to see my buddy Latrice.

My mama got back to working odd jobs just to make ends meet. It wasn't much, but somehow, she made sure we had food to eat. I believe we were one of the poorest families in the neighborhood. She worked from sunup to sundown and I never really saw her do anything else. I never noticed her dating anyone either. Listen, this woman was a true beauty. She had a number eight figure that went on for days. My brother and I knew she was some kind of wonderful. We were destined to one day have a complete family. The households in my neighborhood didn't have many active men living in the home. I bet my mama remained hopeful of one day meeting a nice gentleman.

We had family members that lived nearby. My Aunt Gloria lived in our apartment complex, but she was married. She was a cutie too, a yellow bone with long legs. She was what we called "light skinned" back in the day. My grandma's three daughters, two light skinned and one caramel colored. Aunt Gloria was married to my uncle Donald Ray. I don't remember much about him, other than he was the one who gave me the nickname Bingo.

Most of my family lived nearby and we always had company over. My Aunt Gloria and her son, my cousin Pat, and his sister would come by to see us. His real name is Robert, but we called him by his middle name. Our cousins from Decatur would drop in from time to time. One day there was a knock at the door. Mama answered, and it was her nephew, Cousin Pat, and his friend. They both lived in a house where they rented rooms on East Rosedale Street. Mama kindly let them in, the conversation shifted very quickly, and my cousin Pat didn't get a chance to introduce his friend. This man was some sort of a minister from Baton Rouge, Louisiana. His name was Nathaniel Thomas and he was not handsome at all. His skin was extremely textured and oily, and he had a strange vibe about him. It was like his spirit wasn't quite right! I was around five years old, but I instinctively knew something was off about him.

Cousin Pat later mentioned that things took off with Mama and her new friend. He said he didn't know who did the pursuing, but he saw his aunt taking food over to Mr. Thomas' room. That's what they called him, well, Brother Thomas, to be exact. My brother and I were content with the three of us in the house. We were introduced to Brother Thomas around 1985. Our time alone with our mother quickly changed. You'd think we would have been thrilled about Mama dating a new man. She was happy, as if she'd been struck by Cupid himself.

Days went by and those two grew closer. Brother Thomas would stay late nights over at our home. Around this time my brother was thirteen and I was approaching six. Mama seemed to love her new man. My brother and I, on the other hand, felt the opposite. I think it was because he was taking all her free time away from us. She got so comfortable with him and decided to let him babysit us. She'd go off to bingo and leave us home alone with him.

There was this one day my older cousin Lawanda stopped in for a visit. She was known for dropping in unannounced. I didn't care because she was one of my favorite cousins. She came in to find our apartment quiet, and she walked in to see if anyone was home. As she walked towards Mama's room, she opened the door to find me asleep in the bed with Brother Thomas. She was shocked to see me there sleeping with him. She screamed for me to get up and go with her. Lawanda believed that a young child shouldn't be sleeping with a grown man. I'd later hear stories about how she couldn't stand his very existence. I'm sure Cousin Lawanda mentioned what she saw to my mama. Nothing ever came of it, nor was I questioned about it. He was trouble, and he even made attempts towards Cousin Lawanda. Brother Thomas was beginning to make enemies in Fort Worth and Decatur, Texas. One of those enemies was my great aunt Laura Johnson. If anyone could discern anything, it would be her. I was told that she couldn't stand his guts.

I was also told that family members tried to warn my mama about Brother Thomas, but love is blind. One evening, Mama left me home alone again and she went only God knows where. I was left alone with her boyfriend and I'm not sure where my big brother was. I remember laying on the couch and there were two huge hands around my neck. Brother Thomas was choking me, saying that I better not ever tell anyone what he did. I was raped in my very own home! I'm not sure which room it happened in, but I was sexually assaulted by a man who preached the gospel. He said that if I told anyone, he would kill my mama and my brother. I was so afraid of losing my family, that I kept silent.

A few weeks went by and I was being babysat again by a child rapist. My mama would go about her day with work and her gambling addiction. At night I hated going to sleep because I knew exactly what was going to happen in the morning. Not only did the sun rise, but my little body would get raped by a grown man. On one occasion I was fed up, so I created a plan to try and protect myself. I walked out of my home one morning and sat on the floor in the back seat of my mama's car. I laid there quietly in a fetal position. Let me tell you this, I was trying to save my life from another invasion. As I lay there, I waited for Mama to get inside of her car. I moved a bit, trying to get comfortable, and I made too much noise. Mama heard me, and she ordered me to go back into the house, because she had to get to work.

I shut the huge rusty green car door and walked slowly back to the apartment. Brother Thomas would be waiting in her room. He was a huge man compared to my tiny little six-year-old body. I was thin, very skinny and of course, I hadn't developed at this age. Brother Thomas would always wear white clothing when he wasn't near any pulpit. He certainly wasn't living a godly lifestyle and wasn't anywhere near pure. He would remove his belt and I'd hear the sound of the belt buckle. He would create a lubricant before he raped me. I wasn't aroused or anything, being so young. He decided to use spit from his mouth to coat my vagina. On a few occasions, he would use lotion or Vaseline inside my private area. He would place his penis inside of my vagina until sperm would go everywhere. My body would feel weird and I would feel a numbing sensation. He would lay on his back and hold his penis. I remember him wiping the white liquid off my body and he would get dressed.

This became a regular daily routine in our household. There were times when I would go and play with Latrice and one day, I told her what had happened. I told her that I had a secret to tell her and she sat patiently waiting for me to tell her. I said, "Hey, Trice, you know my mama's boyfriend?" She said yes, and I then told her that he had been messing with me. I decided to tell her more in detail and begged her to never tell anyone.

Now if my memory serves me right, word got out about the abuse and my mother found out about it. She was naïve, and her mind was solely on her man at that time. I wanted him gone but my nightmare had only gotten worse. Nothing really became of the secret getting out about the sexual assault.

One evening my mama came into the living room where my brother and I were sitting, and she was smiling. She sat down beside us and said, "Kids, I have some great news." Mama looked us directly in our faces and said that she and her boyfriend were going to get married. My world seemed to spiral down in an instant. It felt like I was right in the midst of a tornado. She'd known him for about a year. She was the only one happy about the news at that moment. These two hadn't dated long and I was trying to understand why she wanted to take this step. My mind couldn't comprehend why she would want to marry a child rapist who preached the gospel.

You'd think that would have been enough for the day. But Mama went on to say that we were going to move to California. My brother had his reservations about Brother Thomas as well. He didn't like him from the very beginning. My brother was adjusted to being the only male in our house, so I'm sure that is why it bothered him. Now he had to hear about our family moving away. This was heartbreaking for him. He didn't want to leave Texas, nor did I.

When word got out that my mother Joyce was getting married, she didn't have a celebratory committee. To the contrary, many of our family members thought that she was out of her mind. When my Aunt Laura heard the news, it crushed her sweet soul. With all of the negative feelings in the air, you'd think that would have been a clue to rethink the entire marriage proposal. Clearly this wasn't the case. Mama's baby sister Marva was married herself at the time and she was happy for her sister. It was confusing because she had ill feelings about Brother Thomas. She mentioned that she and her husband had loaned money to bury the twins that Mama conceived with Brother Thomas. God had a plan and obviously He didn't allow those babies to be born. In some way, I believe He was protecting them from being raised by such a disturbing and sick man.

As the days progressed, preparation for the wedding was taking place. Mama knew exactly who she wanted to stand by her side on her wedding day. She asked her good friend Linda and her baby sister Marva Glenda to share in the big day. The wedding party consisted of family and close friends. She had flower girls and my brother and I both were included in the wedding. They decided to get married on June thirteen, 1985. The plans were still going ahead but the finances didn't match the vision they had for their wedding. As my family and I began packing for the big move, a financial windfall happened.

I later received word that my cousin Lawanda and her old man, Mr. Greene, had decided to help financially with the wedding. Oh, how I loved them both, but couldn't fathom why they would do that. This was the same cousin who couldn't stand the very idea of Brother Thomas. Why would someone want to contribute to this madness? Did anyone care about the safety of the children who would grow up in the house with this man? The wedding license was filed, and the church was booked. The two lovebirds married in the summer on the West Side of Fort Worth.

THE WEDDING OF JOYCE AND MR. THOMAS
1985 IN FORT WORTH, TEXAS

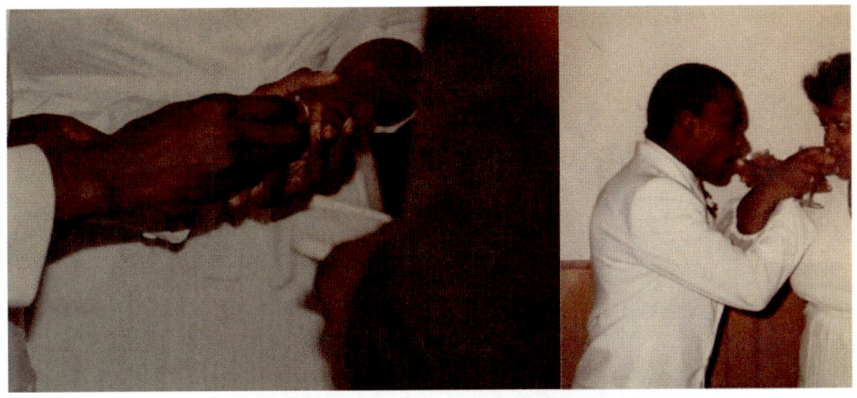

JOCELYN PICTURED HERE WITH BROTHER THOMAS

One the day of the wedding, everything seemed to be extremely hectic. They obviously didn't have a wedding planner because things weren't going smoothly. In fact, everything was out of place; guests were running late, and to top it off, the cake turned over in the car. Our family and friends gathered inside of the church to witness the union. Brother Thomas had his Louisiana family there to support him. My grandma even made an appearance all the way from Munday. It was a very short wedding and we had to witness the agony of taking pictures with our new stepdad. My brother and I had the strangest body language. Our faces told our true feelings of how we felt in that moment. Brother Thomas flew to California shortly after and we stayed behind to say goodbye to our family and friends. I never knew why he went ahead of us, but he apparently had something important to do. My cousin Lawanda picked us up to take us to the airport.

Though they plot evil against you and devise wicked schemes, they cannot succeed.

Psalm 21:11

CHAPTER 3

Beyond the Bay

A journey of heartache, laughter and change.

The signs read *departure flight* as we entered the Dallas Fort Worth airport. We all grabbed our luggage and headed for the ticket counter. As we stepped onto the escalator, I was holding on for dear life. My mama, brother and I walked with my cousin Lawanda and Scotty to get our boarding passes. Everyone was so quiet as we headed to our gate and waited patiently to board. My little cousin Scotty was sitting near my brother and I sat and stared out of the huge glass window. Mama and Lawanda and a family friend were talking grown up stuff. I heard someone say, "Flight 1986, Dallas Fort Worth to Oakland, California, boarding first class passengers." There were a few other letters called aloud and we were next to board. Everyone stood up and gave these massive bear hugs. We boarded the plane and my little cousin cried tremendously as he watched the big jetliner take off into the sky. He yelled out, "Chris, Chris!" with tears streaming down his face.

What was destined for us in Pittsburg, California? As I sat on the plane, it dawned on me that this was our very first plane ride. I sat next to my brother and we ate honey roasted peanuts. Mama had fallen asleep and missed out on her free soda pop and peanuts. Brother and I gazed out the window. The flight was bumpy, and it was frightening, so I closed my eyes and fell asleep on my brother's shoulder. When I woke up, the pilot said, "Welcome to Oakland, California. The temperature is seventy degrees." We had to wait in a long line as our bags came down from the top of the plane. Our luggage was old and beat up.

My brother was wearing his navy blue short with his socks pulled all the way up to his knees. He always seemed to have an alligator on his shirt. Mama and I wore dresses all the way down to our knees. After Mama married Brother Thomas, we couldn't wear jeans anymore. He mentioned that it was a part of his religion. In fact, he had all sort of rules for us. I couldn't wear my hair in one single ponytail and nail polish was out of the question. We walked outside and saw sunny California for the first time and there stood Brother Thomas. I wished and hoped that one day my real father would come and get me. I had to settle for this substance of a male. He was wearing his usual tight white pants and a white t-shirt with a long sleeve shirt. He had coarse kinky hair and his skin was so oily. It grossed me out each time I saw his smirk of a smile and his stench of smelly cologne. At least Mama was happy to see her new husband; after all, they were newlyweds.

We were dreading this new state we had to now call home. Brother and I sat in the back of his dark blue car. As we traveled through Oakland, we saw so many trees, and Brother said they were called palm trees. We made our arrival in Pittsburg, where we would be staying. Our new environment didn't look very appealing. There were huge buildings everywhere, I'd never seen anything like it. Brother Thomas unloaded the car and we headed to the front door of a section of the apartments. A lady greeted us at the door, smiling and with open arms. She introduced herself as Auntie Evelyn. We walked in and I noticed she had kids of her own.

I met her three boys and she had a daughter too. It was nice meeting them, but I was anxious to get settled. She introduced us to her twin boys, and we were kind of close in age. I didn't want to be rude, so we spoke, and we followed her through the apartment. We stopped at the door and she said, "This is your room." I was stunned. *Our room*, I thought. Can you believe that we were going to be living here with people we didn't know? I mean, Brother Thomas knew them, but we didn't. He was leading the way now, and I bet my mama felt like a puppet, she went along with whatever he said. We were residing in the El Pueblo apartments. This was going to be our first home in Pittsburg, California.

OUR FIRST PLACE OF RESIDENCE IN PITTSBURG, CALIFORNIA IN 1985

JOCELYN AND CHRIS IN 1986

(Photoshoot planned by brother Thomas; our mama wasn't included)

I later discovered that Auntie Evelyn and Brother Thomas met at a church in Richmond, California. They initially crossed paths at another church. He asked her if he and his new family could come and live at her place. It was supposed to be on a temporary basis. I don't understand, why in the world someone would marry a woman when they couldn't provide for them financially? Brother Thomas asked if we could stay for two months. He was an assistant pastor and later became a Senior Pastor at a small church in Richmond, California. This would become the church where I'd spend most of my time.

While he was getting acclimated as the new overseer, we had to suffer with our time. As the realization settled in, I thought about my friends in Texas. I missed them terribly and I was miserable. Who would be my best friend now? I didn't know anyone other than our housemates. The summers there in California were pretty cool. Kids played outside, and music was the highlight of it all. I always got lost in the lyrics. The sounds of M.C. Hammer played constantly from our boom box. Now I understand why I fell in love with *Help the Children* by Hammer. I found out that we drove through his hometown Oakland on our way to Pittsburg. I would dance my little heart out when his music played. I met some new ladies who gladly handed over some change to help me get ice cream from the truck. I was beginning to like this place a little bit.

The school year was approaching, and I had to get registered for classes. Brother Thomas took control of everything; my body wasn't the only thing that he took over. We had to adjust and get acquainted with our new surroundings. My brother Chris became cool with Auntie Evelyn's older son. They were closer in age and ended up attending the same school, Pittsburg High School. They were bound to be friends, and they both loved playing football. Me on the other hand, I wanted to get to know Auntie Evelyn's daughter. She was so pretty, and her smile was radiant with those dimples. I'd follow her around and watch her as she curled her hair.

I'd stare as she combed her hair and hoped that I'd style my own hair someday. Sheena was a greater braider too, and she would braid the mess out of someone's hair. When I got older, I learned to braid hair. I was always finding something to do, so I would hang with the twins. Auntie Evelyn's boys were cool, and they didn't mind me tagging along. Everyone called them Fingers and Fats. There is a story behind the nicknames. My Auntie mentioned that when they were babies, Fats would drink his milk and he would then drink his brother's bottle. Fingers would suck his fingers as a baby and that became his name. I fell in love with my new big cousins. The twin brothers were inseparable, and I had become the third wheel. We would go outside and walk through the complex. The others would be out playing football. I never knew where we were headed, I was just happy that I had someone to play with me.

One day, Fats handed me some coins and we knocked on someone's door in the complex. I asked Fingers, "What are we doing here?" He smiled and said, "You'll see." A lady answered the door and she said, "May I help you?" They asked her for a Kool-Aid Frozen Cup and some Now and Laters. It was so cool; we had a store right in the midst of where we lived. They called her the Candy Lady. You could buy all sorts of things like pickles, frozen Kool-Aid and candy. It was a poor kid's dream! She had everything that would ruin your supper and give you a stomachache if you ate too much.

We went back home and sat on the sidewalk and enjoyed our treats. I was a foodie, even back then. I was introduced to a few restaurants called Sizzlers, Togo's and New Mecca. I loved eating at those places, especially New Mecca. I would order bean and cheese dip and chicken tacos. I'd find myself wiggling my little feet at the table. My brother would always be the first to finish eating and he'd finish off the food that I didn't eat. Christopher was like a human vacuum; he sure could put some food away. He could eat for hours and hours. I recall times in Texas at the dinner table when he would be the first to finish his food. I'd sit and stare at my sweet peas because I simply hated them. I was trying to figure out how in the world was I going to swallow those horrible tasting things. Mama would turn her back, and Mikey would eat all of them for me. Back in the seventies a commercial aired that featured a kid named Mikey, who ate a ton of food. It's funny that Mama called him Mikey at times because of his middle name being Michael. I appreciated his appetite because I hated eating vegetables.

Our weekdays were busy in California, it seemed as if we were dressing up for church every other day. We went to church for Bible study and all-night prayer shut-in's. A shut-in was like a sleepover inside of a church. These old people prayed nonstop and starved themselves of food and only had water on those nights. I never understood what it meant to fast.

On the morning after, I'd be so excited because I knew we were going to have breakfast. Sunday morning service seemed to last entirely too long. Brother Thomas would wear his red and white robe and carry his huge Bible into the sanctuary. He acted out his title very seriously. He'd jump around, dancing across the room. The people sitting in the pews would shout and clap as if they were enjoying his message. I was bored out of my mind, so I would go into the restroom. I saw a girl inside washing her hands, so we decided to play in the water. We had our very own splash day in the sink. This mean old lady entered the restroom saying, "What are you all doing?" She was furious and she quickly grabbed us by the arm and began spanking our bottoms. I never played in that restroom again!

BROTHER THOMAS IN PITTSBURG, CALIFORNIA, 1985

As the summer was coming to an end, fear and I got acquainted. I realized that I'd be starting school soon. My new school was called Heights Elementary. The day had arrived, and I got ready for my first day of school. I dressed myself in a purple dress with pink socks up to my knees. Before I could even blink, I was transitioning a few weeks later to a new school. My tenure at this school was so brief, because I was being registered at a new school shortly after, Village Elementary. Before I started my first day at my second new school, I was summoned by Fingers and Fats. They said, "If anyone messes with you, let us know." I was so happy to have a support system. It was like having two more bodyguards. I was afraid that some kids might bully me, and my new family was serious about protecting those they loved.

I got up early for my first day of school. I'm not sure if I was assaulted the night before; my memory would fade away from thoughts of the abuse after so many occurrences. I was thrilled about going to school, so I got dressed in my pink and black striped dress. I wore pink bows in my hair, and I thought I looked cute. I was excited to meet my new teacher and hopefully make some friends. My big brother was in charge of taking me to school. It was cool to know that his school was right next door to mine. He was enrolled at Pittsburg High School. Our mother wanted us close, since he got the duty of dropping me off to school.

Our rides to school were interesting, we would listen to all sorts of rap music and of course he played Too Short. My poor little ears got lost in the beat of the music. When I arrived at my classroom, I was greeted by my teacher. I saw eyes watching me as I searched for my desk. I found it and I noticed that it was in the front of the class. I even had a locker cubby where I could store my backpack. Our morning started with everyone saying their name and some shared stories about their summer. I was so nervous when it was time for me to speak. I was standing at the front of the class and shaking like a wet puppy dog fresh out of the bathtub. After a few moments of silence, I said, "Hello, my name is Jocelyn Willis and I'm from Texas." I wasn't thrilled about being the awkward tall kid towering over everyone in the class. After I spoke, I quickly went to sit down in my chair.

The school bell rang, and it was time for recess. It was the loudest bell I'd ever heard in my life. All the kids lined up to choose what they wanted to play with outside. I had my eyes on the jump rope and I was hoping that I'd get one. It must have been my lucky day, I ended up with a jump rope after all. My little flat feet headed to the playground, and I saw a few girls playing Double Dutch. Out of nowhere, I found some courage and introduced myself. "Hi, my name is Jocelyn, can I play?"

"Sure, I'm Phylethia and this is Nefertari and Tamara." I was so happy that these Cali girls were so cool.

The girls began to jump, and they jumped like professionals. In that moment I knew we were going to get along just fine. We all took turns turning and jumping. I wanted to jump just as fast, but I had crazy legs. My legs and knees were doing their own thing, but hey, I was jumping. We all had a blast and before we knew it, it was time to go back to class.

My first day was filled with a long schedule. I looked up and saw my brother waiting for me at the door. "Brother," I screamed, "guess what?" I couldn't wait to tell him all about my day. My new teacher was Mr. Miller and he was nice. I went on to tell him about the new friends I had met. He didn't seem all that interested, he was anxious to get me home so he could ditch me to be with his girlfriend. He dated this girl named Heather who was very nice. She wasn't the same race as us, but I didn't care. When the two of them hung out, he wanted her all to himself.

Our drive home was short because we didn't live too far from the school. I couldn't wait to tell Mama all about my day. I was a motor mouth; I was talking so fast that she had to slow me down. As I went on about how my day went, she was folding clothes and putting them inside a suitcase. Mama said that she had some news to share with my brother and me. I was nervous because the last time she said that our whole world shook. Mama said that she was packing because we were going to move again soon. Brother Thomas had found a house for us.

I wasn't excited because I had now adjusted to where we were and was happy with our current arrangements. She and I went into the kitchen to prepare something to eat. I had a choice of a grilled cheese sandwich or some ramen noodles. We had huge blocks of cheese and it was hard to melt. My go to was chicken flavored noodles, my cousin Fats had me hooked on them. I always knew when he was around the house, because music would always be playing. He was always listening to music and dancing around the house. I'd hear *M.C. Hammer* and right away, I'd join in with him as he danced. No matter what time or day of the week, someone was always having a house party in El Pueblo. We'd always go outside to play and after dinner get prepared for bed.

The next day at school I got more acquainted with my teacher Mr. Miller. His full name was Derek Miller and he loved teaching and caring for his students. I spoke with Texas slang and he always made sure he corrected me. If I said anything that wasn't correct grammar, he would ask me what it meant. He was strict, but he really had a passion for doing well as a teacher. As we settled into our desks, he mentioned that we had a field trip coming up. I was so excited because this would be my first field trip. We had to make sure that we got our permission slips signed by our parents. Later that day, I met the bully my cousin had warned me that I would meet. This girl was huge, and she was mean. I was afraid and she picked on me as I played during recess.

Her name was Faye, and I couldn't wait to get home to tell Fingers and Fats. When I got into the house, I ran in screaming their names, but no one answered. I went to the back door and Fats was outside working on his bike. He looked at me as if he knew there was something wrong. I told him all about Faye picking on me and he said, "Don't worry, I'll take care of it." I didn't know exactly what that meant but I had a sense of relief. He turned over the bike and he yelled; he had hurt his hand. He had blood coming from his hand and he went inside and ran cold water over it. I was so sad to see him in so much pain.

The very next day as I prepared for school, my brother mentioned that he was going to pick me up. On this day he picked me up on his bike. It didn't bother me; I was just so happy to see my big brother. On Friday at our school they would pop some of the best tasting popcorn. I was such a foodie, so I bought two bags of popcorn. I made sure I went to school with two quarters in my pocket. No one was going to bully me and take my popcorn money. Earlier that same day, I had an unexpected visitor who stopped by my school. I was jumping rope when I noticed a bike outside the gate. I walked a little closer to get a better view of who the kid was. My eyes widened and I realized it was my cousin Fats. I wasn't sure why he came up to my school, but I was happy to see him. He said, "Hey, cousin, where is Faye?"

I said, "Are you talking about Faye Cunningham?"

He replied, "Yes. Where is she?"

I looked all around the playground and she wasn't anywhere in sight. I told him that I didn't see her anywhere, it must have been her lucky day. He said, "Ok, let me know if she bothers you again." I said ok, and he rode away like he was a part of the police department.

Days always flew by at school and Mr. Miller taught in such a distinctive style, he made it fun to keep our attention. The school bell rang for dismissal and I grabbed my popcorn and out the door I went. My brother Chris would be sitting out front on his bike. We were heading home down the sidewalk near School Street. Around this time, we had settled into our new house. It wasn't a new model home, but we made the most of it. My brother was taking us home safely on his bike. I was holding on for dear life as he rode us onto another side of the street onto the sidewalk. Out of nowhere, the bike started to shake a bit as if the ground was rocky. As I held onto his waist, I heard a loud thump. My brother stopped the bike and we got off it. I opened my eyes and he placed his hands-on top of my head. They were covered in blood. He said, "Jocelyn, did you bump your head?"

I didn't answer because I was in shock. I saw the blood and lost it, and I began screaming and crying as the blood was flowing from my head. I heard someone say, "Little girl, let me help you." A lady came out of her house and asked me to come to her. I ran to her and my brother yelled for me to come back to him. The lady was asking me to come inside of her house.

My brother was being very protective. He didn't want to go inside of her house. After she begged us, we went inside, and she placed a wet towel over my head to apply pressure. She was telling my brother that I had hit my head on her tree branch. She went on to say that I wasn't going to be able to make it home riding back on his bike. "I'm going to have to drive her home, "she said. My brother was so scared he didn't know what to do. He agreed to let me ride with her and he rode his bike to the house. When we arrived, my mama and her husband were in the kitchen cooking. We walked in and Mama went crazy when she saw the blood. She was yelling and asking what had happened to me. We all quickly jumped into the car and headed to the hospital. I remember getting so sleepy and I began closing my eyes. I remember Mama shaking me telling me to stay awake. We arrived at Kaiser Permanente Hospital. The doctor said that my head wound was the size of a quarter. I smiled because I thought about the quarters I had earlier to purchase my popcorn. Come to think of it, I never got to eat that popcorn. My wound was on the left side of my head and they had to cut my hair to stich up the injury. It didn't take long for the doctor to finish with me. Finally, we made it to the house after such a crazy and traumatic day. I was so tired but couldn't help but wonder what was going to happen to my brother. He was asked what had happened when we were on the bike. He said that he told me to duck my head down, but I don't remember that. Brother was in big trouble and I'm sure he got a whooping. He made a mistake, but he was still my hero. After a week or two my wound was healed, though I couldn't part my hair on that side of my head.

As we settled in our new home, we always had a lot of company. Our new little family had become known for having cookouts. I thought it was cool because I knew we'd get to see my cousins, and it was great how often they got the chance to spend the night. We had a huge front yard to play in and there was plenty of room for our guests to sleepover. Having my cousins over made the transition easier for me.

Now in our new home, Brother Thomas had plenty of rules for us, and we had to abide by all of them. We also had chores to do each day. Brother had the most because he was the oldest. I remember one time my brother made me stand on top of a chair to wash the dishes and he was yelling, saying I was going to do most of the work. During this, Brother Thomas walked into the room and caught him red handed. There went another punishment for Christopher Michael.

Meanwhile, my mother had found a nice job working at the Navy base and she had to catch the BART train to get there. She rode that train to and from work and her dear sweet husband didn't pick her up. I'm sure he was mastering his grooming plan, being the child sex predator that he was.

While he was preparing sermons, he was figuring out his next wicked attack. Our new house became a predator play land for Brother Thomas. He allowed my brother's girlfriend to sleepover. We had kids coming and going from our house. When my brother's girlfriend Heather slept over, they would always kick me out of the room at nighttime. I can only guess what they were doing. The next morning, I would sneak into his room and steal his chocolate chip cookies. He loved those soft baked cookies and I'd grab a "Rocky" movie to play in the VCR. When the two love birds would leave, I watched movies on his television.

The next day my cousin Fats came over to play and he was wearing his Michael Jackson shirt. He and I were playing in the house and out of nowhere, here comes Brother Thomas with a camera. He always loved taking pictures of us. Fats and I would always try to out smile each other.

A few months went by and we got word that we were getting ready to move yet again. Mama told me that I should get an early start on taking things down from my bedroom wall. As I began taking down my posters, I thought maybe Mama and Brother Thomas couldn't afford the mortgage. He didn't have a real job other than preaching at the church in Richmond. My mother, on the other hand, had a consistent paycheck coming in the house. I thought that when you married someone, things were supposed to be better. I didn't want to move, after all it felt like we'd just moved in.

We had just had my seventh birthday party there with a house full of guests. That was one of the fondest memories I experienced in that house. We had church members and their children at my party. A few of my friends stopped by and my cousins too. Mama had dressed me in a blue dress with huge white polka dots on it. The kids wore party hats and we blew noise makers as we sang *Happy Birthday*. That was one of the happier memories that graced my childhood. We moved a lot and once again we moved to an apartment building. When we pulled up, I looked over at Brother to see his reaction to the new place. I couldn't figure out if he liked it or not. We unloaded the car and got settled into our new place. It was small and had three bedrooms. I went outside as soon as I put my things away.

JOCELYN'S 7TH BIRTHDAY IN OUR HOME IN 1987

"He brought me up also out of a horrible pit, out of the miry clay, and set my feet upon a rock and established my goings."

Psalm 40:2

CHAPTER 4

Uprooted

Uprooted from Sorrow's Chains.

After we moved into our new apartment complex, I'd spend most of my time getting acquainted with our new neighbors. I met a lady by the name of Lanessa, who had a son and a daughter. She was so nice. She wore bright red lipstick and had a figure that went on for days. She was so pretty and kind to me. I met her children and got acquainted with Cassie and Grant, and we hit it off instantly. When the streetlights came on, I got my behind home.

My family and I sat down to enjoy our dinner. Most of the time, we were eating shrimp, fish, and chicken. When we finished our dinner, my brother and I had to do our chores. Brother did most of the work, pretty much all of it. He made sure he helped me with my homework. My brother would yell at me as he taught me how to write my alphabet letters. I always got the letters 'j' and 'g' mixed up.

My mom would come from her room screaming, "Stop yelling at your sister!" He had a temper that would cause me to burst into tears. I'd cry uncontrollably when he yelled and screamed at me. I figured it out, even though it took me a minute. I would be so proud after I accomplished something.

In my down time from my studies, I found other things to keep me busy. I was a weird kid, a loner most of the time. August 29, 1958 was a date I would never forget. It was the day Michael Jackson was born. I'd begged my mama to buy me posters and T-shirts with Michael Jackson on them. She never bought me any of those items, but I knew someone who would. Brother Thomas gave me presents often, and it wasn't even my birthday. I proudly wore the 'Bad' T-shirt he purchased for me.

I'd go to the corner store to buy honey buns and lemon heads to celebrate Michael's birthday. I would find a place to set up my private birthday table with my snacks and Michael Jackson buttons. "Happy Birthday to you," I'd sing, as if Michael Jackson was sitting right there. I'm so happy no one was there to witness that birthday party. I walked into the apartment later on that evening to find my mama and Brother Thomas packing clothes again. I screamed, "Not Again!" Yes, we were moving, but they assured me it wasn't far away. In fact, it was right across the street. We moved directly across from our apartment building. This building had huge palm trees around it, and a gate around the parking lot. We moved to the back of the apartment building. I had my very own room, and Brother did, too.

By this time, making friends was easy for me, and I met a few friends shortly after we moved in. I met two little girls named Corinna and Maria. I saw Maria playing outside, and I went over to talk with her. Maria asked if I wanted to come over to play at her house. "Sure," I said, and off we went, up the stairs. When we walked inside, there was this short little something with pigtails screaming, "Mama! Maria brought some black girl to our house!" She was confused, because she was African American, but not her mother. Her mother was white, and her dad was black. We all became friends, and we hung out at my place. We'd play on my Slip 'N Slide and make snow cones with my Snoopy snow cone maker. Maria couldn't believe I had so many toys. I told her that Brother Thomas bought them. He always gave me great gifts.

One day, we were all playing in the house, and Brother Thomas entered the room. He was smiling as if he had just received a huge church donation. Our house became the playhouse for all my friends. Cassie, Corinna, Maria and her little sister Shamay, would come to visit. My cousins would come over to spend the night, and most of the time they stayed over the longest. Our parents allowed us to have plenty of sleepovers. The days they would come over, Brother Thomas would tell me to go outside to play. He made Maria stay inside, why I didn't know. I thought maybe she got in trouble for something. I would go outdoors and come in for a glass of water, and I'd hear her in the back room, and she was screaming. I was so afraid because I knew that sound, I bet she was getting raped. She continued to come over and she was assaulted again. I don't believe Maria told her mom right away about the abuse she endured. I didn't want any of my friends to get hurt.

I don't understand why no one did any background checks before allowing their kids to sleep over at someone else's home. Why were all these parents so trusting when it came to their children? We thought receiving gifts from this man was awesome. Even though we were young, we always knew something wasn't right about being raped. Fear had stricken me so, to the point I never wanted to speak of it again. I buried the secret, and the secret that my friends and I shared. During our last tenure as a family, things began to get worse. The sexual assault began to evolve. My cousins were now getting abused by Brother Thomas, too.

We never spoke of it to each other. I later found out that they couldn't hold the secret any longer. My friend Corinna lived in the apartment building as well. She was so cool, and we became good friends. Never in my mind did I think, '*Maybe I shouldn't make any more friends.*' My mind blacked out most of the abuse after it occurred. Corinna began spending a lot of time at my apartment. She would eat lunch, and even spend the night, and come over throughout the day. I believe she was being groomed by this monster, too. This man had a sickness beyond anyone's imagination. She had a mother that was stern with her, so I'm not sure how she fell victim to the sexual assault. Now, in my inner circle, including myself, there had been five children raped by this serial rapist. It wasn't just fondling or anything like that. Brother Thomas would use his penis to rape us. He would use spit or lotion to lubricate our private parts. He would rape our innocent little bodies constantly. He would clean off himself and our body to take away the smell. The smell was horrific, and I would lay there wondering, *why would he do this to me?* It became so frequent that as I grew older, I would have triggers in my mind over and over again. The assaults became routine in our house. At ten years old, having sex with a grown man is downright heartbreaking. My mind was so consumed in the act of the molestation, and my body wasn't even developed yet. I didn't have breasts, nor did I have a menstrual cycle. I was robbed of my childhood innocence.

He would have his moments of guilt, because he would come into the house later on that day to give me a new toy that he had purchased from Toys 'R Us. Brother Thomas spent many days preaching at the church. He spent most of his time there, and at the toy store. Things were never getting any better, and my mother was so clueless. She was so low mentally, because he would be emotionally abusive to her. She'd cry when he'd talk down to her as he belittled her. I never had any sympathy for her. We all lived each day, portraying a Christian family. She would work each day at the Navy base, and he'd prepare his sermons. My brother and I attended school regularly. Who knew that all this madness was going on?

We never missed any days of school. You'd think my attendance level would begin to slip, but it didn't. The truth is, school was my escape, and I never had anyone question me about what was going on at our home. My brother would always see me off to school. The school bell would ring for dismissal, and we'd head home. As much time as I'd spend with my big brother, nothing ever crossed my lips—no words at all. I never told him about the sexual assault. My brother was much older than me, so I believed that he wouldn't be much of a target for Brother Thomas. This man wanted young and smaller children to abuse. For some sick reason, he thought that preaching and raping kids would work for him.

Was he ever abused as a child? I often thought about that later in life. Some survivors of childhood rape repeat what they themselves endured as children. But I don't believe that everyone who endured sexual assault as a child will copycat what they experienced. In any case, I certainly didn't agree with what was happening to me in my home. When I grew into an adult, I never had a desire to hurt a child. What happened to me and my friends was just plain wrong. We don't know his reasoning for committing these crimes. For every violent act that he's committed, I hope he has repented. He is a very sick and disturbed man. My brother Chris mentioned to me that on one occasion Brother Thomas tried to rape him, but he wasn't successful. It must have been the grace of God alone that spared him that day.

Brother Thomas preyed on the weak, and he knew he'd be successful at it as a pastor. So many children that were members of his church, I'm sure, fell victim to him as well. Come to think of it, we had a majority of children that attended every service. The church had become trusting, seeing as he presented himself as a man of God. He was an ordained minister, and he received his ordained minister's credentials on June 28, 1981, in Baton Rouge, Louisiana. He received vocational rehabilitation at Earl K. Long Medical Center. I later discovered that there was a chance he was receiving psychological rehabilitation at this very hospital. It's closed down now; they demolished the building in 2015.

Brother Thomas was in the service and he kept pictures in his photo album of his life. He was married prior to marrying my mama. He collected a lot of pictures of children, and he held tight to his belongings. I was so curious about what was inside of his suitcase. I was snooping one day, and I found something while I was looking through his belongings. When he would leave to take on his acting role as a minister, I'd go and open that suitcase that had a can inside. I opened it, and there were tiny little seeds and white, thin, rectangular papers inside. It almost looked like dark green grass. There was one occasion where he had left the door open, and I watched as he licked the little white papers and rolled them with his fingers. That' right, Brother Thomas was a weed head. He smoked constantly.

Brother Thomas kept himself busy as he built his ministerial resume. We traveled a lot with this monster and stayed at crappy motels. One of which was Motel Six. He hosted many revivals where he had ministers in Richmond, California join his efforts. He was awarded a revival certificate of appreciation in 1983. During his free time, he typed poetry as he expressed himself about his wicked ways and some of the things he regretted. Brother Thomas wrote about Jesus, and how he received a touch from Him. He couldn't spell very well, and I'm not sure if he even finished school. He spoke a lot about Jesus being his friend. He went on to say that you will lose your soul in a world of sin.

He had a way with words, because from the pictures in his album, he was a fan of the ladies and the men. As I turned through the pages of his photo album, I'd see a lot of men with writings on the back of each picture. He was interested in men as much as he liked women. Brother Thomas and Mama spent many days and nights at the church in Richmond. The congregation celebrated them like a king and queen. They praised this man as if he was God, and he worked faithfully in the church as if it was his calling.

MY FAMILY GETTING A PICTURE TAKEN BY BROTHER THOMAS
IN 1985

A CHANGE IN MY LIFE

I once was lost in world and so blind,
I could not see that I was very far behind.
I was doing everything that I went it to do,
I was doing thing that could hurt me and love
ones to.
I was going along everything seem alright,
I give no thought to eternal life.But GOD get
tired of my wicked ways,
I begin to have some very dark days.
My mine was so confused, hart haevly burden,
My soul so troubler, from night and day werren
Can't held back the tear as I begin cry,
I stop and thinking of JESUS I look to the sky.
Then I begin to pray,with fear of not knowing what
to say.
With a frind I went to a old time prayer meeting,
they were singing and praying, and the leader was
teaching.
She told me to stan up on my feet, she said tonight
you and JESUS will meet.
She told me to call him, at first I was shame then
I begin to call his name, then it happen I felt a
change.
With a hot flash and my body trimbling, right about
then I lost my memory.
THen when I came though, my songs were new my walk
was to.
I saw thing in a diffrent h change the thing I
had to say.
I found JESUS my life change so much, I found JESUS
and his my frind.
If you don't know JESUS as your frind, you better
find him are you will lose your soul in a world of
SIN.

BY: REV LEE N. THOMAS

A POEM BY BROTHER THOMAS.

I remember the days when he'd make us stay for hours, whether we wanted to or not. We had to put on plastic smiles and be the first family of the church. Who in their right mind would give him a church is beyond me? Brother Thomas worshipped the church as much as he worshipped his favorite white outfit that he wore faithfully. He also wore cologne with a horrible stench. I remember it because I smelt it on my body after each assault. That scent and the sounds of his belt buckle later became constant triggers for me. I never knew how things would escalate on my behalf. We went on to live the role we didn't ask to take.

My friends continued coming over to our house. I recall the very last birthday party I had in Pittsburg, California in 1991. It was going to be a big celebration—or, at least, I thought it was. He put streamers up that hung from the ceiling, and balloons filled the living room. My mom had gotten a cake baked from one of the mothers in the church. It was a two-layered coconut cake. I hate coconut, but it was my mom's favorite. I thought, *why in the world would she choose a coconut cake for me, for my birthday?* I had to pretend as if I enjoyed it. A few of my friends had come over to celebrate with me. Corinna, Shemaya, and Cassie. My cousins didn't show, and that was weird, because they always attended my parties. The party was great, we ate our barbecue, and we danced.

I wore a peach dress with ruffles on it that flared out from the bottom. My friends sat and watched as I opened all my gifts. I got another Snoopy snow cone maker, and a Barbie ice cream maker. I loved all my toys. My friends were amazed at all the cool birthday gifts I received. At what cost, though? How would I have to repay? I was so lost in the moment of that thought I just wanted to play and enjoy my childhood.

The party was coming to an end, and my friends went home. I was so beat from my party that I crashed on my bed in my party dress. I later awakened to my mama hovering over my bed saying, "Get up, Jocelyn." Why was she looking as if she saw a ghost? She was all flustered, and she went and ran me some bathwater. When

I was getting out of the tub, Brother Thomas came in with a brown paper sack. I didn't know what was happening, or why he was holding the sack. There was a container inside. He opened it, and there was white powder inside of a jar. Brother Thomas put the powder inside of my vaginal area. I was so lost and didn't know why he was doing that. He had the same look on his face, just as Mama did. She was close to him, and I'm sure she felt like something was going on. What was he doing? I really didn't know. They must have had words before all of this occurred to allow him to do all of this. I got dressed and went to go see my cousins in El Pueblo. When I got closer to my aunt's house, I saw my cousin Fats.

Something must have been going around, because he had that same look that I saw on my mom and Brother Thomas. He looked really upset. I called out his name, and he yelled out to me. He was so mad that I could barely understand what he was saying. I do recall him saying something about Brother Thomas. There were rumors on the street that he was reported to the authorities by a few parents in the Bay Area. Fats was so mad that he didn't want to talk to me. I went home crying, and I was so clueless when I got home. Everyone was in a panic. My mother looked as if she had just left a funeral. No one was telling me anything. I ran to my room and began to sob on my pillow. I must have cried a river, the next day at school everyone was whispering and calling me names. They were saying, "There's the molested kid." They repeated it until I ran back inside of the classroom.

Later that day, my brother picked me up from school. He passed our house and dropped me off at my Auntie Evelyn's house. He said, "I'll see you later, now go on to Auntie Evelyn's." I hopped out of the car and I watched as he drove away. I went inside, and my auntie was in the kitchen, cooking. I wanted to tell her about my horrible day, but she looked like her day was just as terrible. I didn't see anyone else around that day. I only remember that it was only she and I. I went outside, and Auntie Evelyn came outside. I was wondering if she heard the news about Brother Thomas getting turned in to the police.

She never said anything to me about it. There was something so different about her that day. She looked at me with so much sympathy, and her eyes would fill up with tears. She'd say, "Baby, are you hungry? I made some skrimps." She couldn't say 'shrimp' and out of nowhere, we heard a car pull up, and we both went outside. Oh, my goodness—it was Brother Thomas. He said he was here to pick me up. I saw my auntie turn into a human shield that day. She stretched out her arms as wide as she could over my body. They had words, and she stood there, waiting to see if he'd try something. I was so afraid for him, because I saw with my own eyes how my auntie would fight someone in the street. Brother Thomas walked away and drove off, leaving me there with her. That was a memory that is still so vivid in my mind, because she was the only one who attempted to protect me from this evil man. I later realized it was one of her sons who told her about the abuse. She had already known that day, so that is why she shielded me with her life. I'm not sure what would have happened to me that day if he had taken me. What were his plans? Was he going to have his way with me one last time? I seriously don't know. I do know that my auntie had big plans for Brother Thomas shortly after she found out what he had done to her children. She was in a frantic mood, and she jumped into her car. He was on her radar and she was going to demolish him. As she tried to start her car that day, it wouldn't start.

God was with her in that moment, preventing her from doing His work of vengeance. My Auntie Evelyn is my 'hero' and she has shown me so much growing up. I always felt loved in her presence, and she was a crucial part of the incarceration of Brother Thomas.

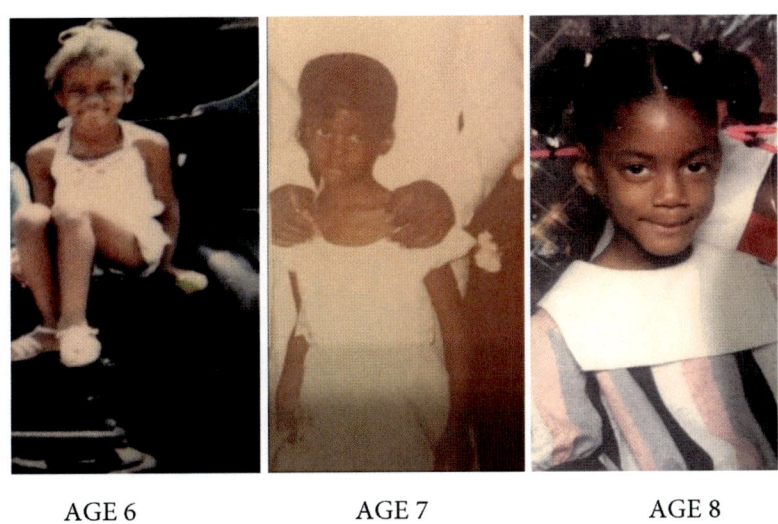

AGE 6   AGE 7   AGE 8

(Sexually Assaulted At These Ages)

AGE 9   AGE 10   AGE 11

(The year I was ripped from the hands of the enemy in 1991)

"The righteous cry out, and the Lord hears them; he delivers them from all their troubles. The Lord is close to the brokenhearted and saves those who are crushed in spirit."

Psalm 34:17-18

CHAPTER 5

Traumatically

I dreamt of my demise.

There was a distinct breeze in the air in the Bay Area. I had awakened quite early to go and sit outside on the porch. This day had such a significance to it, because it was the day I was preparing to say farewell. When I made my way back into the house, I stared at the emptiness that lingered throughout our home. It was quiet. There were no sounds of Shirley Caesar playing in the room. There were no children playing inside our living room. The atmosphere was bare, and the only one I saw was my mama. She was gathering my things and had my breakfast ready on the table. I stared at the black and white checkered tile on the kitchen floor as I sat at the table. I thought about the four places where I'd lived, and now this had become my final destination in Northern California. Mama said we were headed to the airport after we finished our breakfast. She had given away most of my belongings and all I had to take with me was a suitcase. For some reason, I don't remember saying goodbye to my brother or any of my extended family. I'm sure I blocked out most of the memories from my mind. As Mama and I reached the airport, she said that I would have someone assigned to fly with me back to Texas. This person worked for the airline, and she was going to make sure I was safe. After all this time, my mother wanted to protect me. "Flight 1991, Oakland to Dallas Fort Worth, boarding Row C," was announced on the intercom.

Mom gave me a hug, and there was a lady waiting to board the plane with me. I was scared, and deeply saddened to leave the place I had called home for the past six years. I spent six years of my life in Texas as well as six in California, and they both meant a lot to me. Texas had faded away, though, into the back of my heart. The flight attendant handed me a blanket, and I wrapped myself in it. I looked out of the window, and I thought about my school friends and everyone that I was going to miss. I thought about Mr. Miller and my family and my friends. I thought about Maria, Shemaya, and Corinna, the ones who had become my closest friends. Fats was like a brother to me, so I thought about how much I'd miss him. My brother decided to finish school in California, and he was going to later enroll at a college.

The plane journeyed to our destination, and I knew that my life would never be the same without my brother. You know what, it wasn't that I was departing from California, it was that I was leaving without my family. My mom told me that I was going to be okay, and that I'd be living with her younger sister Marva.

My flight landed, and my aunt came to pick me up from the airport. She never knew the truth about why my mom was sending me to live with her. She thought that my mom had a change of heart and wanted us to move back to Texas. As we drove to Fort Worth where she was living, I looked out the window at all of the trees, and finally, we arrived at her home.

I noticed that her street was called Pamela Lane. 1617 was posted right above the front mailbox of her home. We unpacked and got settled, and I was introduced to her husband. She was married to a man named Tommie, and he called out, "Welcome, niece!" I thought, *who is he talking to?* I didn't know him, and this was our first meeting. She walked me inside her house and led me to my new room where I would be staying. Out of nowhere, something flew by me. "Slow down, Pebbles!" she said. My aunt had a dog, and her name was Pebbles. She was wild. She jumped on me, and her tail wiggled back and forth. She was breathing so hard, sounding like she needed some water or something. My aunt pulled her dog from me and told her to settle down. I closed the door and threw myself on the bed, and then I began to cry. Suddenly, I heard the door open, and it was Pebbles. She came over and rested her head on my lap. She was trying to comfort me.

I spent most of my time in my room. Nothing or no one could cheer me up. I was miserable. I disliked being back in Texas. A few weeks had gone by, and on Friday, my new uncle walked in with a little boy. He said, "Hey, niece, this is my son Brandon." Brandon was his youngest son, and we were close in age. He was so little, and I wasn't really interested in making any new friends. I was in a fog, and even though he seemed nice, I didn't want to meet anyone. That didn't last long!

Brandon came to visit on the weekends, and he brought his skateboard over so that he could play. One day, he said, "Hey, you want to push me on my board?" I said, "Okay," and we headed outside, and Pebbles did, too. Brandon hopped on his board, and I pushed him down the street. He was going so fast; Pebbles barely could keep up with him. By the third go-round, Brandon's finger got caught near the wheel, and he hurt his hand. He went running inside the house, and I knew we were in for trouble. My uncle and aunt yelled at us, and we never played outside on that skateboard again.

Whenever you saw Brandon, you would see me. I thought he was the coolest ever, and when he'd come to visit, we'd watch movies and spend most of our time playing outside with the neighborhood kids. We decided that we would have our very own photoshoot with Pebbles. We both fought over who loved her the most and who received the most affection from her. One day, we snapped our pictures on the front porch as we posed with Pebbles. I never knew I would cherish each and every photo that we took together. Brandon was such a loving spirit, and he always expressed his love. He knew how much I love Converse tennis shoes, and he gave me his baby blue Chuck Taylors. I felt like I had won a million dollars! I wore those shoes every day, and I was proud, because my cousin gave those shoes to me.

My Aunt Marva told me that she was going to register me for school at Handley Middle. In that moment, my friends back in California were preparing to attend Central Junior High. I didn't want to attend Handley, or any school, for that matter. If I had to choose, I would prefer going to school with my friends back home. Who would I talk to? I definitely didn't know anyone who went to Handley. My aunt took me school shopping at a used clothing store. She said it was called a thrift store. She took me to get school clothes, and I dreaded that day. We went inside of the store, and she began scanning the racks as if something fashionable would leap right into her hands. She touched a long-sleeved shirt. It was pink and white, and it was a button-down. My aunt grabbed it right away along with a few other items. When we arrived home, she began setting my clothes out for my first day of school. She combed my hair and put a part down the side, and curled it so tight, I looked like I had a mushroom bob. She then placed a gold bow right on the side of the part. I felt like I was fresh out of *the Fresh Prince of Bel-Air's* "*Parents Just Don't Understand*" video. She definitely didn't understand. All I could think about as I stood in the mirror was my Michael Jackson T-shirt and one of my big brother's hairstyles. He would make one huge ponytail and curl my bangs with his fingers. Sadly enough, the first day of school had made its arrival, and I had to walk into that brown brick building with fear chained around my neck and feet. I started crying and tears began hitting my god-awful shirt.

It was a horrifying experience because I felt all alone, and my mom wasn't there, and my brother didn't drop me off that day. I found out that I was going to homeroom, and this was an assigned room for students. It was cold in that room, and my little body began to shiver. I noticed quickly that this school may not be so bad after all. I saw some cuties named Kenneth and Kevin. There were so many girls staring at them as we sat at our desks. I met multiple teachers, and they were pretty cool, too. Mrs. Johnson, Mr. Baker, and Mrs. Moon were my favorites so far. I met all of my teachers and could name them already. I met a girl named Netta; she was from Iran.

After my last period class, my aunt picked me up, and we went home. She told me that later this week that I had to miss school. My aunt said she had to take me to see some people about what happened in California. She said we had to go because it was a requirement, but I really didn't want to go. I didn't know what to expect. I knew there were rumors that were surfing around Texas. I didn't know what was going to happen once we got there. My mother never questioned my brother, and she never questioned me. She acted cowardly and packed up everything and shipped me off to Texas. She said she wanted to protect us, so that is why I was sent away to go live with my aunt. Too little, too late. I was robbed of my childhood. Now, there I was, sitting in a small room, waiting to talk with a couple of strangers.

I heard sounds from the door, and someone was coming in. The woman asked me a variety of questions. I sat quietly, and she waited for my response. Shortly after that, her response was very quiet, and our time together was over. I'm assuming the information shared was all that she needed to give to the authorities. The ride home was very long, and it was very silent. I don't believe my aunt knew exactly how to talk to me. She never asked why I was sent to live with her. My poor little body began numbing the abuse from my past.

I went on to attend school regularly, and I really did enjoy attending school. My grades, on the other hand, were suffering. I struggled through school, and learning was very difficult for me. My mindset wasn't absorbing the knowledge that the teachers were teaching. My worst subject ever was mathematics. I would wonder about my academics and think that my abuse had some effect on my learning. There were days I thought my eyesight played a factor in my learning abilities. I ended up going to summer school one year at Morningside Middle. I had to go in order to be promoted to the next grade. However, even in the midst of failing grades and numbness and rollercoaster emotions, I found comfort in my friendships. I began really good friendships with Licia, Drew, and Veena at school. We all hung out at different times. The word 'trouble' defined us when we'd get together. Rebellion was starting to surface in my life at that time. I was wearing long shorts and tees because I was a tomboy, for real. It's funny, though, I still had a love for make-up. I would sneak off and apply it before school.

There was this one particular morning where my nosy uncle was watching me leave the house. He called out, "Niece! What do you have on your face?" I politely said, "Nothing, just make-up." He was just about to burst, because he couldn't wait to tell my aunt. I couldn't stand him at times. He was so messy and fake and to top it all off, I witnessed him fight my aunt right in front of me. It was after Mama moved back to Texas, and she had to pull him off of her. He lost all cool points with me after that day. He had a few good moments, though. When we'd take long road trips, for example. One year, he rented a van, and we traveled to Louisiana. Can you believe my family and I went to see my brother play football? I was so excited. My new favorite cousin Brandon came too. I couldn't wait. We were going to have a great time. I loved Big Man. That was Brandon's nickname. The van was so huge, it held so many people. The funniest memories about those trips were my Aunt Gloria talking the entire way there. She would ramble on about how gifted she was with so many talents, and it drove us nuts. We really did enjoy our family road trips. We finally ended up in Lafayette, Louisiana. We parked at the hotel where we would be staying the night. My family and I were all dressed in blue and gold, the colors of the San Jose Spartans. My brother played strong safety, and he was a good football player.

I remember we'd all sit in the football stands cheering for him. I couldn't wait until the game was over, because I would get to see my brother. We didn't get to see him much other than attending his college games. My brother was always so excited to see us. After the game he would meet us back at our hotel room, and we'd hang out a minute before dinner. My brother was tall, and extremely handsome. He didn't look like the young boy I saw last in California. He had huge ambitions, too. He studied criminology at San Jose State, but football was his life. Sadly, he never saw those dreams flourish the way he wanted them to. I was crushed when I realized that some dreams really don't come true. I was still a young person, preparing to begin my freshman year in high school. During my last year in junior high, my friends and I discussed our ideas about which high school we would attend. Most of my friends went to Eastern Hills High School. A few of us decided to go another route. My friend Nicky had her heart set out on going to Eastern Hills. She was very smart, and I'd never met anyone like her before. Nicky was so kind, and very popular. There were popular kids in school who were really mean to me. I recall a time where a kid told me that when I grew up, I was going to be beautiful. My heart sank, and I felt like chopped liver. Nicky wasn't cruel, she was different. Her name was Dominique Nicole Hurd but she went by Nicky. She always smiled and shared laughs with me.

Nicky never met a stranger, and I was amazed at how she shared her love with the world, including me. The school year was ending, and she came over to sign my yearbook. Nicky asked if she could borrow it, and she'd return it later that summer. I loaned it to her, and we said goodbye. Summers were cool, because I'd spend most of my time with Lili, Veena, or Drew, or my cousin, Brandon. Drew lived around the corner from me. Lili enrolled a little later at Handley, but we all grew close. We finally decided on which high school we'd attend. Lili, Veena, and I decided on Green B. Trimble Technical High School. It was a trade school. My friends planned on attending to get an education, but my mindset was on the boys. Earlier that year, I went on a work-school-study day at the high school, and I saw all the cuties there. I knew that this was the school for me! They had a cosmetology program, and I loved doing hair, so I wanted to enroll at that school. My friends and I said our goodbyes before our new school year. I kept nagging and nagging my mom about making an appointment with the principal to discuss my future there. Mama gave in, and we met with the principal. The principal looked over at me and said, "Your grades are really poor." He didn't have to tell me that. If I were smart at anything, it was my mouth. He mentioned that if he let me attend his school, I would have to work really hard to bring my grades up.

I wanted to go there and do the best that I could. There were many things that I learned; for one, if I wanted money, I was going to have to earn it. I was just fourteen when I began cleaning houses for money. My mom worked at a health center, and she asked around in hopes of finding a job for me. She found a couple and said that they were partners, and I was going to clean their home for them. I thought, "*Hmm, partners. Oh, okay, sure, I will.*" I didn't care what they were. I wanted to work hard and do a good job. I purchased my very first pair of Michael Jordan tennis shoes. I was proud of myself, and no one helped me earn the money.

By this time, I'd had a few encounters with my birth father, and they were very brief. If he gave me anything, it wasn't anything financial. I was trying to better myself at becoming a hard worker, because I saw my mom work so hard. I wanted a better life, and she wasn't going to give it to me. I swear August rolled around and I was preparing for my first day of high school. I laid my white jeans out and my yellow Tommy Hilfiger shirt on the bed. I thought I'd wear my Jordan's, but you know, I pulled out my baby blue Chuck's. My hair was fresh. My stylist was named Shanette, and back then, I only paid $25 for a wash and style. My hair was cut short at the top, and diagonal in the back. What was I thinking, cutting my hair like that? It was cute though! My first day was cool. I found all my classes and had to learn my way around the school.

It was amazing to be at the school I had dreamt of attending. High School was tough. The workload was massive. We had assignments left and right. My getaway for sweet relief was right up the street at Burger King or Eddie's Chicken. I wanted to eat out every day. The way my mom's funds were set up, it wasn't happening. I decided that I needed a real job to earn money. I started a new job at a place called Digital Dial Communications. It was a telemarketing company, and it was easy money. I got paid weekly to talk on the phone. Being employed meant new clothes, new hairstyles, and fast food.

My priorities were screwed up, but I didn't have anyone guiding me. My mama worked so much, and I saw her only every so often. It was good for me at times, because it meant I could really have some fun. My friend Drew always heard about the coolest parties. She invited me to a party at the Howard Johnson Hotel. Most of our friends called it the 'HoJo' for short. It was a code word so our parents wouldn't know. I met at her house to leave for the party, and I thought I looked cool, pretty fashionable. I wore cross-colored long shorts, and a long-sleeve shirt. I thought I was dope. Drew quickly went into her closet, grabbed an outfit and said, "Go, quick, and put this on." I came out looking like I was about to walk the streets. When we arrived at the party, I was getting looks left and right from everyone. When the DJ would play my favorite song, you know I had to rush to the dance floor.

I was dancing for a minute by myself, and before long, I had two to three guys wanting to dance. When the night ended, I had tons of little pieces of paper with phone numbers on them in my pocket. I was amazed! I had them throwing their numbers at me left and right. Maybe this dressing sexy thing was cool after all. I never thought I'd get that kind of reaction. The acceleration of my life was speeding faster than I ever expected.

"And we know that all things work together for good to them that love God, to them who are called according to his purpose."

Romans 8:28

CHAPTER 6

Embodied Devastation

Shattered glass within my heartbeat.

High School had become my playground. While everyone was hitting the books, I treated that time period like my drug of choice. It meant nothing, I used it to pass the time. I was trying to keep my past from surfacing in my mind. You know, it worked perfectly for a few years. I was skipping school and hanging out with older guys. During my first year in high school, nothing mattered to me. My friends and I would leave school to go hang with two guys named Jason and Chauncey. We'd sneak out of the school, and they'd be waiting right in front to pick us up. My girl Veena was with me that day, and we were headed to the liquor store. Jason pulled inside a car wash directly across from the store, and he left the car running. The guys jumped out, telling us to wait inside the car. I didn't know what was going on. Suddenly, I heard the store employee screaming, "Stop, stop!" and the guys were running with cases of beer in their hands. We fled the scene and parked inside of Jason's garage. It was a rush for me, and I didn't think anything of it. I sat back and enjoyed a few beers with my friends. My young mind was twisted, and it didn't occur to me how things were going to play out.

The next day at school, I would brag about all the mischief we had gotten into. My friends were always talking about their nights at this club called 'Mid-Point.' I wasn't really interested, because you had to be twenty-one years old to get in. Well, where there was a will, there was a way. I got a fake ID, and later that night I got dressed in a halter top and wore a skirt. I put a bunch of makeup on my face to appear older. That did it.

I got in the club, and it became a regular hangout spot. Long Island iced tea had become my new signature drink. I danced all night long until the DJ would tell us it was time to go. My friends from junior high hung out at the club regularly too. Why weren't our parents finding any of this out? I don't know. I was living the high life without getting in trouble. I was introduced to cigars, and they became my new thing. I would buy them and share with my friends.

In between the partying and drinking, I attended cosmetology school. I finally found something positive to focus on. I adored going to class, learning about roller sets, perms, and finger waves. Our instructor allowed us to get our hair styled while in class. I was excited to go to room 275. I loved going to class, especially on Fridays, which had become my new most anticipated day.

My girl Lili introduced me to her cousin, Jennifer, and we hung out after school. I ended up back on the South Side of Fort Worth, Texas. We rolled down the street as we jammed to our music, playing Scarface, and we ended up on a street called Lanty. The neighborhood seemed quiet, but that was far from the truth. As we got out of the car, I noticed a lot of vehicles parked at this one house. As we entered the house, you would have thought it was a smoke shop, because the smoke hit us straight in the face. The girls and I sat down, and I was introduced to a few people. I met this guy named Terry, and as soon as I saw him, I was mesmerized. He was tall and very muscular with a nice smile. I wanted to get to know this man.

We sat and we had drinks, and noticed people going in and out of the house. I didn't know what was going on, but when we left, I was told it was the spot. The spot was another name for a drug house. Crazy enough, every Friday, we'd make our way back to the spot. We stepped it up a notch, though. We'd go dressed up with our hair freshly styled. I had my heart set on running into Terry's fine behind. Around this time, I was seventeen and my hormones were all over the place. By the summertime that year, we'd go to swim and fight parties, which was literally watching a boxing match on TV while enjoying food and of course, alcohol. We became familiar with the local neighborhood drink called 'Blue Monday.' This drink was mixed with Rum and Sprite, and blue food coloring. The men in the room were all twenty-seven and older. I'd sit on the couch and watch the fight and I saw Terry make his grand entrance into the room. The women were thirsty, and it wasn't for a drink. They wanted him, and I could relate. I was favored in his eyes, because he came right to me, and greeted me with a hug. I was doomed for hatred, and those women wanted to make it known how jealous they were. I was turning up with those drinks when I noticed Lili and Jennifer had changed their clothes. They said that they overheard the girls talking about ganging up to cut my face. I sobered up and got myself together. Moments later, Terry found out, and cursed the women.

He grabbed my hand, and we headed down the stairs to the van. The ladies followed us as we began driving really recklessly, and we almost had an accident. Finally, Terry and I made it to our destination at the hotel, and I told my friends goodbye. This had to have been our second time spending the night together. Terry wasn't officially my guy, but in my mind, he was. Any time we hung out, it meant only one thing, and that was sex. He was popular, and just about everyone wanted him.

You'd think I would be focused on school during this time, but my mind was far from it. I was getting all these assignments that had me bored out of my wits. My teacher had given us a writing assignment; we were asked to compose an essay. I hated English and I wasn't very good at writing. I thought to myself, my *grammar isn't very good, nor is my spelling.* I committed to the assignment, but it was excruciating to write that essay. My heart really wasn't in it, and I didn't care if I failed or not. I continued to put my academics on the backburner. It was easily done, because my mama wasn't too concerned about my education. My grades were failing, and she was failing at parenting. She wasn't alone, though. My birth father was exempt from my life. I would see him every blue moon, when I'd go to visit him, or he would stop by and pick me up. At the time I was interested in learning more about him and his children. I thought it would be cool to have siblings.

He was successful at having children with multiple women. I believe it is around six of them. For some strange reason, I believe there are more children out there somewhere. When I got introduced to his children, I was very young, and it was nice to meet them. He has four girls and two boys who all lived in Texas. During this time, I was in high school, but I spent most of my time on the South Side, enjoying the street life. Back then, I was completely numb. My birth father was married to a lady named Anne, and she must have been something special. When I met her, I thought her intentions were pure, and at the time, maybe they were. You know, they say kids can discern the aura of an individual. Well, they truly can. She wanted me to call her anything but 'Anne,' and my mama was furious. She told me that I better call her by her name.

Anyway, after all that I had endured, I was thrilled to learn that I had a huge family in Texas. However, that feeling quickly came to an end. After all the partying, I felt myself needing something more. I met a guy named Derrick, and he was my first love. He was the sweetest guy I had have ever met. He was tall and high-yellow with a beautiful smile. We dated for a while and became very close. Derrick and I hung out all the time. It was pure puppy love, and I never wanted to leave his side. We spent many days arguing, but we made up like nothing had ever happened. He would always call to check on me and make sure I was okay.

I fell in love with him, we were so young and didn't know what love was. My heart was lost in his, and deep down, he cared for me. We hung out in Forest Hill, and his friends knew that I was Red's girl, that was his nickname. I was cool with his friends, and we became like family. One day, we were all in the street, playing, and someone threw a ball toward me. I ran to catch it, and it landed in my chest. Derrick was furious, because he said I shouldn't have been playing with them. He was concerned about my heart condition. Derrick learned about my heart murmur one evening when we were in an embrace. He was holding me and asked why I was so nervous. He thought I was afraid of him, because my heart was beating tremendously fast. I hated telling him that I had a heart murmur, but I just had to. He was so concerned from then on. I truly loved the way he loved me. Our story was beautiful, and we dated for a long time without being sexually active. I'm assuming that is why he felt the need to cheat on me.

Derrick came over one day and said that he had something to tell me. He let me know that he was getting ready to be a dad. I was hurt, and I couldn't look at him the same ever again. As he told me the news, I could see the tears in his eyes. I believe that was my first embodied devastation while in a relationship. I hated the news of his infidelity, so I knew what I had to do. I went back to the club, and it was called "*The 20 Grand.*" It was a cool spot on the South Side of Fort Worth.

It was a hole in the wall type of club. It was small, and my girls and I hung out just to post up. I'd run into Terry, and he'd always have a pick-me-up that got me through. My girl Jennifer would make sure that she'd get me ready for the night, because we knew by the end of the night where we would all end up. By this time, our inner circle was growing, and it wasn't with adults. My friends were having babies, and I wasn't. God had some other plan for me, because I never got pregnant. Not even once. I would get asked a few times we'd hang out, "When are you going to have kids?" and I'd laugh, saying, "I don't need them." I never understood what they meant by that. I never realized that maybe I had a purpose, and God knew exactly what that was.

My mom would encourage me to go visit my birth father from time to time. I wasn't interested, I felt like he should come to visit me. I became angry because he wasn't what I visualized in my mind. I thought he was going to be this loving and strong person. My feelings were all over the place, and my past came back to reintroduce itself. I began having nightmares, and I was so furious.

There were nights where nothing could soothe me. The partying, the drinking, the sex wasn't working. My past was very present, and it was chasing me down. I had triggers that surfaced just about every day. I hated the sound of belt buckles, and I would dream about the rape. I was growing cold, and I wanted to embrace death. I would cry rivers just about each and every night.

I began hating my parents for not protecting me. I was angry at God for allowing my body to get raped for years. One day, I was in a low place, I wanted my life to end in that very moment. No one was my lifeline, and my family was pouring salt in my wounds. I thought about suicide, but I could never see myself doing it. I was already in hell, and I heard that it would be an eternal home for me if I killed myself. I had to think of something, so I remembered the prayer my Aunt Laura recited when we would pray. I began calling out to God for help. I pleaded with Him, and I begged Him to save me from my current destruction. I was consumed with the feelings of sex, and I engaged myself in it, whether it was with someone or just by myself. I was hurting, and I needed another outlet. One evening, as I rested upon my bed, I decided to write what I was feeling in that moment. I felt like I had taken pain relievers, but it was just through writing. Writing had become my new high, and I was excited to write again. When the triggers would come, I'd grab my notebook, and I would write. My writings were dark and cold. It was my new baby, and I got lost in it. My writing was my voice, it was my medicine. I wasn't expressing myself verbally, but I was writing what happened to me in my notebook. I began writing poems and short stories. I wrote about being the child of a single parent and decided to share it with my birth father. He was outraged, so he decided to write me a letter.

I went to check my mail one evening and saw it was a letter from Mr. Tollie. He had to let me know how he felt about my poem, and he went on to say that he never wanted to be a father and have kids with my mother. He said that his kids were smart, and I not only have a hole in my heart, but in my head. I was devastated! I fell to the floor and cried like an infant. Luckily, I had someone at my home. His name was Kelvin. I now know that God was with me even in that moment. I saw my birth father in a different light on that day.

My misery was increasing, and when I looked up, my senior year was here staring at me. My final year. I managed to pass all of my classes. We had to take so many tests in our final year. One particular test, we had to pass three sections. I was terrible at it. I went to tutoring, and I tried my best to get a high score on that test. I conquered two out of three. I didn't succeed, and I didn't graduate with my class. My life was dancing in sorrow, and no one was reaching out but God. I toughed it out and went to the graduation to see my friends graduate. I believe I grew acquainted with depression shortly after high school. During the summer, I was dating two guys around the same time, and all I did was attend block parties. They were my new thing. We would hang out and dance until the snap of bullets would soar through the air. I was running for my life, and I always got away. The gunshots were a regular thing at the club spots where we would congregate.

I became immune to it. Nothing—and I mean nothing—scared me. Everyone I went to school with was working or going to college. My mindset wasn't on any of that. I was being successful in the numbness. Periodically, I'd catch up with my old friends from junior high. On one occasion, I got an opportunity to speak with my friend Nicky. She was in town from college visiting her family.

Nicky and I hadn't spoken since middle school. She mentioned to me that she wanted to meet up before she returned to Arkansas. It was so great hearing her voice. She was so cool, still the same amazing girl that I remembered. It was so thoughtful that even though she was down visiting her family, she wanted to make time to see me. God always wanted to give me added joy even in the midst of my troubles. As we talked on the phone, I imagined her lovely smile and her kindness. I truly loved her, and I was looking forward to seeing her again.

My summers consisted of kicking it in Dallas and hanging out with my friends. I spent most of my days doing hair for cash, and since I didn't have a job, I was pretty good at it. I learned a few things during cosmetology class. There were some days where I was so tired and didn't know if I really wanted to finish with the whole cosmetology thing. I found out there was some type of mix-up with our instructor's credentials and our hours. I was told I wasn't going to receive a majority of my clocked cosmetology hours. I wasn't deeply disappointed, however, because my passion for styling hair was fading. Yet, despite my feelings, I wanted to finish what I started.

I began a new season in my life after high school. I spent most of my mornings sleeping past noon. One morning, my neighbor, Celeste, kept calling my cell phone. I rolled over to answer it. "Hello?" I said.

Celeste said, "Girl, there is someone knocking on your door, and he won't stop. He's been out there knocking for a while now." I wasn't expecting anyone so early in the morning. Well, it was early in my eyes even though it was almost noon. I pulled myself out of the bed, walked to the front door and peeked out to see who it was. I was upset that someone was knocking as if it was an emergency. I simmered down when I discovered it was my good friend Billy. He and I met at the Fort Worth Zoo when we were teens working during the summer. We were friends, but our affections went far beyond that. He was adopted, and I wished that I could have been in his shoes. Billy was a kind person, but his demons haunted him for some reason. A lot of the men I fell for had a connection with crime. When I opened the door, he was smiling and hugged me so tight. He mentioned that he had been recently released from jail. Billy and I stayed in touch through letters and cards. He expressed how painful his life had been and professed his love for me.

I was longing for something, and I found a token of it in him. Let me explain. You see, just about every guy I went out with tried to push up on me. Billy was just the opposite. He treated me with so much respect, I found it odd that he was called a womanizer. We spent a lot of time together. Our pain strangely bonded us. Billy and I were never involved sexually, our relationship went far beyond that. We were friends but acted as if we were in a relationship. I was so fed up with him one day and asked him, "Why don't you want to be in a relationship with me?"

He replied, "I don't want to hurt you."

I didn't understand what he meant. I was deeply in love with him, and I wanted us to be official. Billy and I had our moments of intimacy, but he'd always stop before we went any further. I felt so low in those moments. I later realized the respect and love he truly had in his heart for me. He was something special, and he made it known that I was too. For instance, nearly beating on my door for me to answer, he didn't give up. As we stood in the doorway embracing, I had to literally pull away to get a breath in. He had some friends waiting out in the car and I told him to invite them in. We sat and caught up, and I was so happy to see him that I forgot how busted up I was looking. Billy loved me unconditionally, naturally pretty. During my time with him, I looked over and saw a camera sitting on the dinner table.

I began snapping shots as if we were doing a real live photoshoot. After we spent time catching up, I walked him to the front door. As we went outside, he hugged me as if I'd never see him again. We took a final picture, and he hugged me tightly again. I thought he was just being overly affectionate. He said, "Hey, J, I'm going to make a stop, and I'll be back."

"They that sow in tears shall reap in joy."

Psalm 126:5

CHAPTER 7

The Rising of Resilience

She rose through the cement of sorrow.

A few days had passed, and I thought that it was odd that I hadn't heard from Billy. I reached over to grab my cell to see if I had any missed text messages. My phone rang shortly after, and I rushed to see if it was Billy calling. I answered, and our mutual friend was calling to tell me that Billy was murdered. I completely lost it, and I couldn't believe what I was hearing. I felt it in my spirit, though. The one person who truly loved me with a great depth of compassion was gone. I wept and my soul was in agony in that moment. I didn't get any sleep during the next few nights. The only thing I could think about was how empty I felt inside. I reached for my pen and my journal and began to write about the love that I had for my friend and the bond we shared. As I held my pen, the tears would saturate my page, and I would have to start again. My mind reflected backwards to the pain I endured just two years prior.

I never got the chance to see Nicky when she was in town. She was murdered in Pine Bluff, Arkansas; I was asked to read a poem that I wrote about her. I didn't know at the time, but God was preparing me to comfort those in need through my writing. I was so nervous, but I walked up to the microphone and I did it. I began with, "Nicky was a shining light in a world so black…" I had never spoken in front of an audience. My body was shaking, and my voice was trembling, but I got through it. I was so very proud of myself, and I knew Nicky was smiling on me in that moment. She is now resting peacefully in my heart.

I thought I was losing my mind after I heard of Billy Barrett's passing. I had to do something to hold myself together. I lit a candle and I laid in my bed and watched the flames. The candle had writing on it and it read, but love goes on forever. I experienced a very memorable and vivid dream that night. He spoke to me in the dream, and he wanted to remind me that our love would be preserved forever. Billy reminded me to read his words of expression that he shared on each card that he sent to me. My eyes began to open slowly as tears started to flow onto my pillow. I got dressed the next day, and my cousin and I went to pay our respects. I had to pry myself out of the seat to walk to the front of the church. It took a while before I actually got up. I thought about how well loved he was as others spoke about him. That was it, I had to get up and share my heart. I would picture his smile as I read about the person that he was to me. I remembered the love that we shared and how he held me as if he never wanted to let me go. I truly loved him, and his love for me was—and still is—present with me. In his words to me, "True love is a promise spoken heart to heart. But you know, love… love goes on forever."

From that day on I kept writing and my words went from grief to anger. I was writing daily as I tried to get past my grief. I thought about those who meant so much to me. By this time in my life, I had written and spoken at three of my friends' funerals. I was writing three years prior to that. I was losing those who truly loved me. Nicky, Billy, and Ashlyn were all taken so soon. Ashlyn was a brother figure in my life, and he and his grandmother left this world way too soon. I remember it like it was yesterday. I was being loved by God and by them. I simply adored Ashlyn and his grandmother. I was at home sleeping when I woke up and heard the news. I heard Ashlyn's name and that is how I discovered his passing. I was furious with God. Why did they leave earth on my birthday? I thought that God was ripping my heart from me. Ashlyn was such a beautiful spirit, and he was well loved. He and I met through a mutual friend, and we hit it off quickly. His personality was so contagious, and you could get lost in his energy. Many people called him 'A.D.'; for Ashlyn Dickens. There was one thing I adored most about him, and it was how he truly wanted the best for me. Ashlyn was a very hard worker, and he was very family oriented. He treated me as if I was his very own family. We spent many Sunday mornings going to church together. He shared his grandmother, and boy, did she love me. Ashlyn's grandmother's name was Ms. Adele. She was the sweetest, and she didn't play. When we were all in church, we had to focus, and we couldn't horse around. Ashlyn and his grandmother were like my extended family, and I loved them dearly. The people who had shown me so much love were gone. I felt a great abundance of love from these two humans.

I wrestled with, could I write a tribute about my love for them? I did, and there I was speaking before another audience of mourners. Jesus, what are you doing? I questioned God, because I wanted answers. God didn't answer me in that moment, but I was reunited in my dreams with my dear friend and brother, Ashlyn. He appeared in my dreams to comfort me and to let me know that he was okay. He also had a message for me to relay to his mother. I called her the very next day, and she was happy to know that her son sent a comforting reassurance. I had a piece of comfort, but my heart was experiencing so much grief. I was trying to figure out, how was I going to get beyond the pain of it all? I knew about God and His power, but it felt like He was failing me. My life was in shambles, I didn't want to live, and I wanted to see my friends again.

My past was having its way with me, and I became deeply lost in alcohol. I began drinking heavily but it never gave me any relief. I was so familiar with drinking alcohol and hanging out in the streets. All these things were my numbing agent. I wasn't ready to submit to joining a church, but I was willing to visit. I decided that I would join my mother at a church she had been visiting. I went, and it was a really nice church. The church was filled with the Holy Spirit. I gave it a try a couple of times and decided that I would one day join. I was only nineteen at the time, but each time that I entered the building, I was drawn to the worship.

Everyone was very friendly and greeted you at the door. I noticed that the worship had me at a place of peace. I would meet God at church, and it didn't even bother me that I was back in a place where my faith had been shaken. Not this church exactly, just to be in church was courageous of me. The minister that taught and preached the word of God was Bishop Richard E. Young. He was a small man in stature, but when he preached, I swear it seemed like he grew taller. The way the word was spoken through this powerful man of God spoke to my ailing spirit. In those moments, I believe that God was using His word to begin my healing journey. I remember sitting in the sanctuary, and all my pain seemed to fade. Sadly, when I went back home, it reappeared and surfaced again. I truly believed in the power of God's word, but I felt like it was ineffective.

I was struggling tremendously. I was desperately desiring to be free from my past terrors. I needed more worship and God's word. I needed a touch from God Himself to heal me. I continued to attend the church, but I still felt like I needed something more. The Lord always knows how to direct our steps. I can't recall exactly how I came across this place called the Women's Center, but I'm so glad that I did. I was seeking help, and the Women's Center offered rape and victim services. They introduced me to a lady named Lynn Guy. She was going to be my counselor. God knew there was a great need, especially in the African American community.

I remember when I was introduced to Lynn, I was so nervous. I didn't know what to expect from her, and I prayed about it. I prayed that she could help me. During our first sessions together, I asked her, "Do you think I could get better?" and she said, "I wouldn't be in this profession if I didn't think that was possible." Lynn didn't delve directly into my past, she wanted to address my present first. She asked me what was currently hurting me the most, and all I could think about was Billy. She asked me to talk about him and write a letter to him. I remember writing the letter, and she told me to tell him how I was feeling. I finished the letter, and I had to say my final goodbye. I felt a great weight lifted from me. I had mourned his death for quite some time. Lynn had a way of assisting with my peace. I was very grateful for her, and I made sure God knew how thankful I truly was.

Around this time, I was trying to make sense of my life. I wanted to do something with it, and maybe that was because everyone seemed to be so doubtful about my potential. I was good at styling hair, and I made money doing hair at home. After giving it some thought, I made my decision to go back to school and finish my cosmetology hours. I was so excited that I was making steps towards healing and also establishing a new career. God was opening doors for me and making everything happen. I never thought that my heart disability would help me get financial help with my tuition.

I was thrilled when I learned that I didn't have to pay anything towards my tuition. My tuition and my student kit were all paid in full. This was just the push I needed to stay focused. I made pretty good grades and made a lot of friends. The way we worked on the clinic floor was liberating. I was doing roller sets and finger waves on all those little ladies so fast. I thought I was a pro when it came to roller sets. I wanted to finish school, and I was determined to finish strong, and I told myself that I could do it. On the inside, deep down, there was something more that was brewing within me. I had a desire for make-up artistry as well as modeling, so I enrolled at Barbizon Modeling School. I was attending two schools at once, and honey, let me tell you that I was a proud young woman. Things seemed to be looking up for me. I was well on my way towards discovering my purpose, or so I thought.

Sunday mornings always came around really fast. In between my counseling sessions on Tuesdays, I looked forward towards attending church at The Chosen Vessel Cathedral. Jesus would meet me each time I was there, and I got busy serving in the church. The love that I felt from the ladies who would greet me as I entered the building was beautiful, so I decided that I wanted to be a part of it. The ministry was called the Greeters Ministry. I was given a purple suit, and I'd stand in the lobby to welcome the guests and the members.

Shortly after, I decided to volunteer in the youth department, I assisted with Sunday school and took care of the children. I was asked by Brother Rayford if I would be willing to become a children's church director. I was hesitant at the beginning, but I humbly accepted, and I served under the ministry for three years. However, after the praise and worship, the music would stop, and my demons would haunt me. I remember the scent that reminded me of my abuser. My dreams were pure terror, and I simply disliked falling asleep. I decided that I'd do a longer session with Lynn to get the help that I needed. There was something urging me to talk with her more, and then I decided that I wanted to talk with my pastor about my decision. I scheduled an appointment with him, I brought items in to show him, and put them on the table. We sat down, and he asked me what the documents were that I had on the table. I told him that they were pictures and the ministerial license of my ex-stepfather, who raped me as a child. He looked at them for a while, and he told me that he didn't believe that I was going to need any more counseling. He went on to say God was going to heal me and set me free. I didn't know how to feel or what to think in that moment. I explained to him that I was hurting, and I was unsure of why my mom didn't leave him sooner. He encouraged me, and I headed home. Later that night, Jesus spoke so clearly, saying, "I'm going to set you free."

I wasn't sure if what I was hearing was correct. I wasn't used to hearing the voice of the Lord. My ears were so new to His voice. I drifted off to sleep, and I rested so peacefully that night. I awakened to the sun peeking through the window. I had a desire to pick up my pen and begin writing. I wrote all about what was ailing in my soul. I was much more together with my words on that particular day. I didn't have any other place to put my words but in my notebook.

Out of nowhere, I heard a knock at the door, and it was my good friend Dontel. He was stopping by to see if I was free to hang out. I met Dontel at Little Sam's detail shop one summer while I was hanging with my friends. He and I became so close and we spent so much time together. He was one of the sweetest guys ever. He was fighting his own battle though. His battle was a health issue called Sickle Cell Anemia. He never complained about what he was going through. Dontel was so kind-hearted, and he'd give you the shirt off his back. One day, I was so afraid to stay at my home because it had been burglarized, and he came over just so that I wouldn't be scared. He told me that he didn't know what he would do if anything happened to me. Dontel said that he was going to stay with me, and we both fell asleep on the couch. Our friendship was so beautiful, and when he was ill, I made sure I'd go see him in the hospital. I brought him his favorite snacks and we'd lay in his hospital bed and talk for hours. Even though he was sick, our time together meant a lot.

It was almost time; graduation was drawing near. Can you guess who was there to meet me on my last day of school? It was Dontel, he was smiling so big, and he told me constantly how proud he was of my accomplishments. I simply adored this man and I pray he knew that! He made me sad when he'd always talk about his demise, and it would hurt me terribly. He told me he wanted women to carry him while he laid in his casket, and he wanted me to write a poem and speak at his funeral. Sadly, that never came to be. I never got the chance to say goodbye to Dontel. He passed away, and it was as if every force in the world didn't want me to attend his home-going service. I made peace with it after I gave it much thought. I knew that if I attended his funeral, my grieving would have been extremely massive. I held tight to his love and preserved everything we shared in my heart. He always reminded me that I wasn't just another girl. Even during that time, I felt as if I was being buried alive, but somehow, I was capable of rising above it. I know he'd be so proud of me.

The summer was fast approaching, and I had to prepare for my state board exam. I was so nervous, and God and I had plenty of conversations. I knew He'd see me through, but fear was kicking my butt. I didn't want to fail, and I just had to show those who spoke against me, that I could truly make it. I had to succeed and pass my test. I studied with my instructor Rebecca, and she gave me the business. After all the hard work, I traveled to Austin to execute my exam. I had to do a haircut and demonstrate a manicure. It was one thing after another. Three o'clock rolled around, and I made it through the test. I felt like a weight was lifted from my shoulders. I called my Aunt Gloria, and she reassured me that I passed the test. She was a hairstylist herself, and she knew I had passed. Maybe God spoke a word to tell her that I had did just that. I made it back home after staying the night in Austin. I was so happy to be home.

My mom was anxious to know how I did on my exam. I was so thrilled to tell her all about it. She smiled as I shared every aspect of the exam. We were already rejoicing, because I completed something positive in my life. What truly amazed me was how fast the results came in the mail. It was on a Saturday, to be exact, when I opened the letter. I was super anxious to get inside the envelope.

"Dear Jocelyn Willis, you have successfully completed the state board operator's examination." In that moment, I was rising with resilience.

"No weapon formed against you shall prosper."

– Isaiah 54:17

CHAPTER 8

Tragedy to Triumph

The weapon formed, but it wasn't prosperous.

The seasons began to change, and fall overshadowed me with a warm greeting. I was preparing, and I had a few leads for employment. I wasn't excited about styling hair anymore, and I needed a job. I did some research, and I reached out to a local day spa. I was pleasantly surprised when the receptionist mentioned they were hiring. The open position wasn't for a stylist, it was for a shampoo technician. I was so anxious, and I needed the money, so I jumped at the opportunity. They called me back for an interview, and can you believe I got the job? My supervisor was a gentleman by the name of Tim, and he was the sweetest guy. I became acclimated to the protocol and procedures of the salon. My immediate coworkers were also assistants to the hairstylists. It was so nice to meet Rosie, Karen, and Sylvia. The pay was good, and the tips were amazing. I made so many tips and I used them for splurging. I was a beast at assisting those stylists with their clients. I was becoming popular, and the clients began requesting me to shampoo their hair. We would talk about our lives, and shared intimate things with each other. I was getting comfortable at my job, and I was really focused on bettering myself. I didn't need any distractions in my life. On weekends, I'd spend time with my family. My immediate family was extremely small, and I would visit them and hang out at their house. I was so young and couldn't see the forest for the trees.

One day, I got introduced to a man who was related to one of my relatives. I was so young and naïve. I fell for it, and there went my focus. I began dating this guy, and we became close extremely fast. Things started to evolve, so we decided to make it official. He was so nice, and we spent a lot of time together. He had been the first love I embraced after the demise of all of my closet friends. He was in the Army Reserve, and he was very ambitious. The beginning of our relationship was lovely, and we both were believers of God. I was saving myself for marriage, and so was he, we truly wanted to honor God with our bodies. Tony was on the same page with me, that meant everything, and I didn't want to disappoint my Lord and Savior. One evening, however, things got heated, and we ended up falling short, and we had sex. We repented so hard afterwards, and we prayed heavily. I wanted God to forgive me for breaking my promise to Him.

The relationship continued and we grew closer as we got to know each other. Tony began doing the sweetest things for me, and I fell for him. He started visiting my church, and he decided to join. I was in love—or at least I thought I was. In my mind, I thought in some way, God had sent me an earthly love after all the heartache and pain. Our relationship was blossoming, and we made many attempts to stay celibate. For some reason, we couldn't shake the friction and love was brewing between us. I discovered that lust had become a factor and it soon grew into an addiction.

We were becoming one through sexual intercourse, and we battled the spirit of guilt. This man and I were consumed with ungodly desire and we knew it was wrong. We crossed our boundaries, and I was very sorrowful for it. There were many days I had to sweep our sinful nature to the back of my mind and embrace the love that we shared. Many times, love can be disguised with something else, but for me, it was truly love. We had so many people rooting for us, and a few that were against us. We spent time talking about the future and what we wanted for our lives. He mentioned to me on many occasions that he was going to marry me. I was elated, but never thought he was serious until he in fact asked me to marry him.

We were so happy to tell everyone that we started to plan our wedding. Family members had their say about it, and Tony began to digest their negativity. The relative that introduced us was like a snake in the grass. She was a huge factor and displayed strife most of the time. This woman was always getting involved in family members' relationships, including mine. Our short-lived engagement didn't last very long, but it was long enough for my heart, mind, and soul to become tarnished. My phone rang one evening, and it was Tony on the line. He was telling me that we needed to talk, and that he needed some space. In that moment, he pulled the plug from my heart. This man not only called off the engagement, but he ended our relationship over the phone. I was numb, extremely numb in that moment.

The relationship was over just like that, and I sank deeply into depression. I reached out to Bishop Richard E. Young. I remember as if it was yesterday. I slowly walked into his office. He greeted me, and I sat down in front of his desk. He said, "Daughter, how may I help you?" I let out the biggest stream of tears you could have ever seen. His face began turning red, and he was trying to fight back his own tears. He handed me a Kleenex, and I began telling him what had occurred. He was furious, and he really wanted me to stop crying. The man, who I knew as my spiritual father, had become my dad. I was going to get through this, he told me. "You're going to get through this. You will love again." In that moment, I didn't understand what he meant. He also said, "The right man is going to come along, and it's going to last."

That was the very last thing I wanted to hear. Hearing the word 'love' in that moment was like pouring salt in my wound. I was facing another tragedy, but God knew, even in that moment, I was going to overcome. It's funny how one experience can remind you of all the other hurtful things that you've experienced. I asked my dad, "Why did I have to endure so much? Why was my birth father absent from my life?" Dad went on to tell me that we share in the sufferings of Christ. He told me to let him know what was going on in my life and that when I hurt, he hurts. I truly believe that God gave me an irreplaceable angel on earth.

I have a heart of gratitude for him. From that point on, he became a beacon of light in my life. God made sure that I not only would receive an agape love from God Himself, but He gave me someone heroic in Bishop Richard E. Young. I was growing despite everything I had endured. It took me a long time to get past the devastation of the broken engagement. I began focusing on my writing. I used it as a tool from God to usher me to a place of holistic healing. The Lord was giving me a talent that would later change my life for the better. I would spend my weekends at Barnes & Noble. I camped out there. It was like my second home. The bookstore had become my sanctuary. I would walk throughout the store and dream my little heart out. I'd make my way to the poetry section of the store and stare at the book covers of Dr. Maya Angelou. There was a book that stood out to me, it was entitled, *I Know Why the Caged Bird Sings*. I knew that title meant something profound, and I was going to discover its definition. It felt like this book was choosing me. I would gaze upon the pages as I got lost in the story. Who was this woman? She was so radiant. She had to be someone special to have written so many books. I decided to learn more about this woman of virtue, and I stumbled across her poetry book that made my heart leap. Dr. Maya Angelou made me feel like I was the most beautiful girl in the world. I believed I could conquer anything. I started gaining courage to become a published writer.

I was consumed with the book "*I Know Why the Caged Bird Sings.*" My eyes opened wider and my heart shivered when I read the chapters. My soul was resting within the pages of her book. It was ironic that the author was raped, just like me. As a result of it, she became silent and was mute for a very long time. I sobbed profusely as I read her story. I became familiar with the essence of her spirit as I read her books. In my mind, she had become my godmother, and I had hopes of meeting her one day. She was blessed with so many talents, and I truly admired that about her. We had so much in common. I knew that one day I would write and publish a powerful piece of work. I didn't know exactly how or when, but I knew I would do it.

My first love had always been modeling. I was so tall and awkward looking; I would dream beyond my environment. I visualized myself walking the runway. I had big dreams, and I would practice walking any chance I got. My body was thin, and I mean scary thin. I lacked curves, and I didn't have an upper half. My mother was so fortunate to have large breasts. I didn't get that portion of favor. After modeling school, I went on to pursue my dream. One day, I decided to try out for a reality show. The show was hosted by my favorite supermodel of all time, Tyra Banks. After watching a few episodes, I was anxious and decided to try out. I had to record an audition tape to be considered for the show. Unfortunately, my self-esteem was low, but I pressed past it anyway.

I thought I would make it through. A small part of me felt like I could succeed as a fashion model. I wanted to model couture gowns and rock the runway in hip-hop gear. My tomboy era wouldn't vanish. The day I tried to record my video for the audition, all hell broke loose. I remember standing in the hotel lobby, full of light and energy. I stood up, and I said, "Hi, my name is Jocelyn Willis, and I'm America's Next Top Model." Out of nowhere, I started gasping for air. I was trying to catch my breath. My friends ran over to see what was wrong with me. It was so weird. I was nervous or something. I couldn't understand what was going on. I pushed my way past it all and managed to finish the taping of the video. My good friend Derick loaned me his camera to record the video. He had always been such a positive and supportive friend. When we got the video completed, what were the odds of anything else happening? I tried to take the tape out of the camera. The tape wouldn't eject out of the camera, and we were so afraid of what was going to happen next. I decided to take the camera to my mother's job and see if I could get some assistance. No luck. Derick thought that it was so odd, because he had never had anything happen to him while he used his camera. I became familiar once again with the adversary. I never got the opportunity to submit my audition tape. My dreams of modeling were crushed. I was so overwhelmed and discouraged and out the window went my dream.

I went back to what I knew best, and that was my writing. My pen would write the words that were in my soul. I felt worthless, and I was reminded of the words that were written by my birth father. Satan took every opportunity to push me closer to despair and misery. It was terrible, and I started to believe him. I tried to overcome his voice, but it didn't happen instantly. God intervened and reminded me constantly of how valuable I was through His word. God was leading me closer to His word and further away from the negativity that had lain dormant within my mind. God was up to something, and I didn't know what He was doing in my life. My days and nights would consist of tears, agony, and isolation. The seeds sown in my life had taken root, and my poetry was increasing. I made a few trips to the bookstore to purchase journals and diaries. My voice was leaping from the pages in my notebook. God was quiet during those times. I was beginning to think that He wasn't listening to me. I was this young, African American girl who was searching for help. I wanted someone to tell me that I was beautiful. I needed someone to give me the love that I didn't receive as a child from my parents. I wanted to fall asleep after writing most of the night. Through the pain and shedding of my tears, I had hopes of never waking up again. I turned to my weakness and embraced it. I came across this guy named Len. He was handsome, tall and he rode on a motorcycle.

I was needing some type of attention, and I thought he was it. Len approached me at a funeral home while I was attending a wake of one of our mutual friends who had passed away. He walked up to me as if I was the cutest thing ever. "Hi, my name is Len," he said, and I was smiling right along with him. We quickly exchanged numbers. Len walked away, and my friends were giving me the details about who he was. He was very popular in the street community. I was blown away by the fact that he was interested in little old me. I went on to embrace the desires of my heart at that time. I was so serious about making money, but I wanted to be in a relationship as well. This man called my phone shortly after we met. When I think of it, we never—and I mean never—went out on a date. Len was known for his work ethic, and he was very good with his hands. I was a true witness to that. I spent most of my weekends at his house. I was so stupidly naïve to allow myself to stoop that low. Len never truly committed himself to me, and I knew that. I was in a place of despair, and I was one of the many women with whom he was spending time. He was possessive and had his demons. Len was much older than me, and he loved the club. This man made sure he was on the scene at any and every given time. I fell quickly for this man, and for no apparent reason. Why would I want to be with someone like that? I was yearning for something that I didn't get as a young person. I wanted to be in an exclusive relationship with him.

He wasn't ready to give me what I wanted, nor what I needed. Len was ready for something and it wasn't a commitment. He was willing to have intercourse. I remember one night not using protection while having sex. That next day, I felt so guilty and upset with myself. I had to let out my frustration, so I shared it with someone. I received a lecture about how stupid I was. I felt so convicted in my spirit. My mind began running wild. I was so nervous about contracting a sexually transmitted disease. Len wasn't loyal to me, so I had to get myself tested. I panicked as I waited for my results and thank goodness, I received good news. I sat there on the couch and I heard the words *get it together.* There was a requirement that I had to watch a video. It was a video about motherhood, abortion and adoption. It never dawned on me that I could be pregnant. I was so focused on the idea of contracting a sexually transmitted disease. I heard a soft voice say, "Ms. Willis? The doctor will see you now." The doctor shared with me that I was not pregnant. I was ecstatic and relieved. In that moment, God had graced my life again. I was so grateful to God, even though I had failed Him. I was so thankful that I wasn't going to be a mother. As time progressed, I began having flashbacks about my life. My life wasn't moving in the direction that I had hoped for. I simply had to make a decision. I need to make a change. I had a long road ahead of me, and I knew it wasn't going to be easy. I made a decision to end the fling that I had with Len.

It was time for us to call it quits. I wanted to put everything behind me, especially the fornication and being involved with street men. I knew that God would restore my life. I wanted a man of substance, and I had to make room for him. I needed a man of God, a true, authentic man of God. It felt as if I was getting pushed closer to a relationship with Jesus. During my times of getting to know Him in a greater way, He was leading me to write my heart's desire. My writing became very therapeutic during some difficult seasons in my life. I wrote about what was haunting me. I found myself sharing my most intimate feelings. I would grab my pen and notebook and words began to flow. My steps were ordered by the Lord and He allowed me to serve in my community. I was asked to write for families who had lost loved ones. It was easy for me to comfort someone else's loss through their times of sorrow.

My writing continued to progress, and I began writing for weddings and funerals. God was using me to bring light to others, and I was compensated for my work. I was amazed because my work began to increase. I was writing so much for others that I began to put my journal writing on hold. I remember when I was younger, I heard older folks say, "You'll understand it better by and by." God was preparing something greater for me. I was thinking about how I could use my gifts in a greater way. I desired to make a greater impact, and I wanted to get hired to write. I was led to contact a funeral home to share my work with them. I made an appointment to speak with the director of Pencer's Funeral Home. Unfortunately, that never came to be. A few weeks after we spoke, he was murdered.

"A man's gift maketh room for him,
and bringeth him before great men."

Proverbs 18:16

CHAPTER 9

Pieces of my Passion

Stir Up the Gift.

By the time I was in my twenties, I had discovered a greater love for my passion. God was building me piece by piece as He introduced me to a whole new era of my God-given gifts. The steps of a good person are ordered by the Lord. Jesus knew how to direct me in the right direction. I found myself cleaning out my storage that was filled with boxes of poems and short stories. As I read the poems, I began thinking about what I should do with them. Now, let me tell you, when you ask God a question, be ready for a response. I met a lady at my church who served in our church bookstore. This woman had it all together with her gifts. I watched as she would talk about the books that she had written. I was amazed at the fact that she had written so many books. I was thrilled as I listened intently. She told me how she got started publishing her books, and how she did it all herself. I asked her if she could guide me in the direction I should go. I didn't know where to start. Ms. Maggie politely agreed to help me with publishing my book. I was so excited that I wanted to dance like King David. Later that day, I went home, and I compiled my writings together and started to outline my chapters. God was moving, and He didn't let me waste any time, not one minute. When God has you on an assignment, you better embrace it and walk by faith. As I prepared for bed later that night, God gave me visions about my book. He gave me the title *'Let God Love You Past Your Pain.'* I believed that God was going to restore me. As I began to write my book, Jesus was working. I picked up my pen, and it was like God was writing through me each step of the way.

As I wrote my introduction, a calmness came over me. I spoke about the sorrow that was on the inside of me. God was holding my pen, and the Holy Spirit was guiding me. I recall a time when I had to stop writing to gather my thoughts. It felt like I was going through a cleansing of some sort. At the beginning, I wrote about what was hurting me the most. God was pulling the layers back as I held my pen for dear life. My life was unfolding through the pages of my notebook. God was ministering to me as I shared my soul with Him. There were moments where I thought, *I'll never finish this book.* I had poems I had previously written that I wanted to put in my book. There was something that God wanted to birth through me. I can gracefully say that I am so thankful that He was there with me. God was using the gift inside of me to usher me to a place of wholeness. The book I was writing was going to be used to help other sexual assault survivors get past their pain. This book was strategically set in place to be used as a holistic form of restoration. God was showing me that He was in complete control of my life. During the process of writing my book, I was being tested at every hand. Satan was in position trying to stop the release of my first book. God was equipping me with His grace to see me through. I was determined to finish what I started. I had to finish no matter what would come my way. I wrote when I was tired, hurting and angry. I was embracing endurance and perseverance. God was filling me with tenacity and consistency. No one in my family had modeled that in my presence.

I never saw anyone go after anything they desired in life. Writing had become my passion, and it was who I could confide in. I spoke to God through my writing when no one was listening. I completed my book, and I had to pause a minute, and stand still in that moment. I accomplished a dream that I didn't realize was within me. I was so elated and proud of myself. It was a wonderful milestone. God was so pleased, and I knew if it wasn't for Him, I wouldn't have finished my book. Lord, God, I thank You for holding my hand and writing through me. Jesus knows exactly what we need, He gives insight about what we can do through Him. It wasn't in my strength alone but in the power of Jesus Christ. Prayer played a factor in the process of writing my book. I wanted to pay tribute to my Savior. God was my strength and He propelled me to complete my book.

I WAS SEXUALLY ASSAULTED AT FIVE YEARS OLD AT MY
CHILDHOOD HOME IN 1985.

STANDING IN FRONT OF MY CHILDHOOD HOME IN 2016.

Jesus had given me a vision for my book cover. My
photographer captured the vision beautifully. I sat in a dark room
and kneeled as I closed my eyes to pray. That was it – I was saying a
prayer. This was the concept for my book cover. A light was shining
on me, and Jesus was the light. God was the light shining on me in
my darkness. Christ was a beacon of light that saw me past my pain.

God loved me past my streams of sorrow. He was the ray of light that guided me out of the bondage. As soon as my book cover was printed, I framed it. I was ecstatic! I marveled at the idea of my poetry being shared. I was the product of fatherlessness, rape and poverty, and I published a book. The completion of this book meant something more than my internal manifestation of healing. It symbolized that I could do anything. I was being groomed for a journey bigger than I could comprehend. God works in mysterious ways, and I am blessed to be used by Him. We are so fortunate to be a part of His purpose and plan. God included me in His will, and He wanted me to be His next dimension of glory. Just to think that God included me, Jocelyn Ja'Net, in His will, is amazingly wonderful.

After I framed my book cover, I had to share it with my dad. I rang the doorbell to his office and waited patiently. I was so excited that the anticipation was rushing through me. I walked inside and noticed him sitting at his desk. I was smiling as I pulled my frame out of my bag. I handed it over to him, and he held it up a minute.

He began to read it, and before I knew it, we both had huge smiles on our faces. He said, "Is this for me?" I smiled and said, "Yes." Bishop Richard E. Young was proud of me. He asked me how I felt about this accomplishment. I was talking nonstop about the process. He has been an inspiration in my life. I had to include him in my book, he wrote the most beautiful foreword. I'll always have him forever in my heart and preserved in my book. His words meant the world to me. He was such a significant part of my healing. God used him to usher me to the very place I was standing in, and that was redemption. I recall him asking me, "Daughter, are you truly healed from your past?" and I replied, "Yes, sir, I am." His concern was a genuine love from a father figure. As I walked to the door of his office, he said these words, "Daughter, I expect great things from you." Those words pierced my heart, and they remain tattooed in my soul. I truly believe how powerful words can touch your life. Words have suffocated me, and some have caused me to rise above it all. Maybe God was clearing every word curse that had been sown in my life. No matter where I journeyed, I was being directed towards greatness. My steps were being ordered every time I got up from a fall.

After the completion of my book, I was anxious to go to the bookstore. I spent most of my time in the autobiography section. I was interested in reading about stories of those who had overcome extreme odds. My story alone was filled with so much. I always knew that one day, I'd see my books on those shelves. I was ready to tell my story. I couldn't get enough of reading autobiographies and watching documentaries. I didn't think it was strange, it was something that caught my interest.

Praying was significant in my life. My heart desired to cover in prayer, I ended up registering for a free conference number. My prayer line was established because I wanted to intercede for humanity. I chose the route of social media to bring it to pass. Social media was so popular, and I thought about creating a private group page as well. God surfaced again, giving me the name *'Sisters with Stories.'* I wanted this online platform to be a place where individuals could share their stories. Sisters with Stories was a great platform where I could encourage others. Women began joining the group, and it was beautiful, I was being blessed because of it. I wanted my group page centered around Jesus Christ. I'd host weekly prayer and conference calls within the page. God was very present during these prayer calls. I interviewed guests on the conference line. God was fueling me with so much vision about my newfound ministry. I was focused solely on prayer, and He was leading me to do so much more.

I didn't want to have an ordinary look for my group page. I came across this phenomenal lady online by the name of Grace. She displayed her work on Facebook. I wasn't afraid to ask her for help. I politely reached out to her, explaining my mission for Sisters with Stories. Grace was interested in my idea, and she designed four logos for me. I was so happy that day. She gave me so much motivation and I went further with the vision.

God was ushering me to launch out into the deep. I was a few months away from releasing my new sisterhood. I wanted to do more, and I felt a tugging in my spirit. The creativity on the inside of me was flourishing. Three months after the launch, I decided to create a space to bond with the ladies. We had connected online, and it was time for us to meet. I was so swamped with the planning, and I was very nervous. I prepared for my very first meet and greet. I was praying for a great turnout. I had a plan of incorporating food, jewelry, and make-up. I thought that this would be a good approach, an effective way to get the women there. The women came out to support me and the energy felt great. The turnout was much more than I had expected. I smiled in the essence of seeing the ladies interact. I was onto something, and I didn't know exactly what was in store for Sisters with Stories. God was anointing my hands to do amazing things in the community. My confidence was growing by leaps and bounds. I was jotting down ideas about future events and outings.

Although serving was near and dear to my heart, I had a greater love for writing. I was learning to balance my time. On many nights, I'd listen to music to help the sting of loneliness. I wanted to meet someone special, but I had my fears. God summoned me again to pick up my pen, and that's what I did. I didn't realize that He was using my gift of writing to help me believe in love again. I began writing down my thoughts and feelings. I held my pen so tightly that the words were flowing onto the pages. I wrote to God about what I wanted in a man. My heart was speaking for me through my short stories and poetry. I asked for a man of God, someone of substance. God had given me the title for my next book. I entitled it 'Prophetic Love Revelations.' The writing was designed for those with extreme optimism. I decided to write this book to help others. There was one thing I hadn't written about, and it was love. Love had been so cruel to me in the past, I wanted nothing to do with it. Yet I was commanded to write this book. Maybe in some way, God was giving me the desire again, but I truly had to embrace it. At the conclusion of writing my book, I was praying for an idea for the book cover. I asked for guidance for the concept of the cover, and God answered quickly. I envisioned red roses and green grass. I was embracing a man while sitting on the flowers. Now, who was going to be the perfect man to capture my vision? I called a friend and she said she knew the perfect guy for the project.

I was so nervous about asking him to be a part of my book. Sheldon and I partnered in the past in the Dallas / Fort Worth community. I supported his organization on many occasions. It was a great experience to see the hand of God in his life. God was connecting me with people of virtue. I never understood why He was allowing me to cross paths with such greatness. Sheldon allowed me to cover in prayer on his conference call. We later teamed up to feed and clothe the homeless a few times. Sheldon was so handsome and amazingly talented. He was a former NFL player, and he started a nonprofit organization. We met at church one day, and that's how everything began with our partnership. I knew he was someone special and out of my league. Our connection remained professional. I finally got the nerve to call him and ask if he would be willing to grace the cover of my book. His words were so profound, and I was blown away by his response. He quickly accepted my invitation, and I told him that I would fill him in on all the details. I hung up the telephone and screamed at the top of my lungs: "Lord, God, what are you doing?" There was God again, showing up and giving me a little nugget of favor. I had a deadline, and I wanted to capture the book cover as soon as possible. Sheldon was a busy man and I didn't want to waste his time. I set a date and gave him all the details.

The concept of the book shoot was one thing, bringing it to life was something quite different. I was calling around, trying to get prices for rose petals, costumes, and props. I was trying to keep my sanity, and it wasn't working. I needed to create a Hollywood love scene right smack in the heart of Arlington, Texas. I just knew I could pull it off. God had given me the vision and I had to do it. There was so much to do! I needed clothing for the shoot. I managed to squeeze some time in to shop.

I was making my way down the aisle of the department store when I stopped and smiled. I was shopping for Sheldon, and I was tickled. Yes, this man was handsome, but I was trying to keep it kingdom. I found a nice pair of khaki pants, and I needed a white t-shirt. The vision was going to be so marvelously beautiful once we embodied it. I walked a few steps towards the women's section, and I stumbled upon my dress. Right away, I said to myself, "That's it! That's the dress." It was a baby doll dress, all white with spaghetti straps.

On my way home, I had thoughts of how the shoot would turn out. While preparing for my book shoot, I had all kinds of ideas brewing within my heart. I was amazed most days at the capacity of what I could hold inside of my head. Even though I had so much going on, I wanted to do something special for some great kids. God placed a specific family on my heart. I knew of a family who had huge dreams. The family consisted of two little boys who simply adored football.

They also had a little sister who was cute as a button. I decided to reach out to a few of my community partners who were former NFL football players. I also emailed a local news reporter who I felt could truly bless their lives. I wrote my vision down, and after I explained it to them, they gladly accepted my invitation. I was thrilled about the idea that would manifest brilliantly. The day before my book shoot had finally arrived, and I was a bit nervous. I asked my sisters of Sisters with Stories to join me as a support system. They were so excited about my shoot. We stacked hay on top of each other out in the bright, green grass, and placed the red petals on top of the white cloth that was on the ground. We had wooden bowls and antique pitchers in place for the gleaning of the weed. It was like a scene from a romantic movie. Earlier that morning, I met Sheldon at a McDonald's that was nearby the shoot area. I had a pep talk with myself and said, "Girl, this is all about kingdom business, and time is money." Thank God I did, because when he walked in, I nearly fainted. Let me put it this way: he is physically fit. I knew I had to behave myself, because I had work to do. After we changed into our biblical attire for the Ruth and Boaz scene, we headed over to the shoot. I had to figure out a way to do two scenes without having to go for a wardrobe change. I figured we could wear our modern-day look under our biblical costumes.

The grass was so beautiful, as the greenery meshed with the red rose petals. I explained to Sheldon that we were going to do two looks. He seemed a little bashful at first. I wanted him to be as comfortable as possible. He truly embraced the character of Boaz, and I conquered Ruth. We were having fun as we prepared for the love scene. Sheldon and I had to embrace one another, and he seemed a little nervous. Sheldon was informed about the embrace right on the spot. I sat on the rose petals and asked him to join me. He was being such a gentleman, and I was willing to help him devour his bashfulness.

"Most assuredly, I say to you, he who believes in Me, the works that I do he will do also; and greater works than these he will do, because I go to My Father."

– John 14:12

CHAPTER 10

Ja'Net: God's Gracious Gift

Multiple Streams of Wonder.

The conclusion of the *Prophetic Love Revelations* photoshoot had surfaced. I sat up on the rose petals with Sheldon, and I heard my photographer Rebecca say, "We're almost there."

As I rested my body between his, I closed my eyes. I truly got into character and prayed for a great shot. I wanted my book cover to scream love. I gently lifted my head from his chest, but my sisters demanded that I remain still. They acted as if they were watching a real-life love story in that moment. I wanted to say, "Behave, ladies!" We finally got the shots that we needed, and we wrapped everything up.

I was proud of myself for not letting my nerves get in the way. I followed through with the vision that God had given me. I wrote a love-based book and shot the cover with a well-known public figure. Later that day, I found myself thinking about Sheldon. Why was I being favored in this way? Why was God giving me this temple to birth out so much for His kingdom? I held my pillow tight as I began to weep. Oh, but wait—that wasn't the only thing that was going through my mind. For some reason, I began thinking about the conversation I had with Sheldon earlier that morning. I was reflecting on our time together on the set of my book shoot. What in the world was going on with me? Was I having a chemistry reaction, like actors experience after a scene? The next few days were simply horrible. I couldn't get this man off my mind. I was miserable, and I didn't know what to do. I followed up with Sheldon by giving him a call. He wasn't answering or returning my texts.

I hadn't seen or talked with him since the photoshoot. I was confused in that moment. I realigned my focus and completed my book. I pushed the thoughts of Sheldon to the backburner. My phone would sometimes be my saving grace. My typesetter, Scott, would call to check on me. He wanted to see where I was with my book. At that time, I was on the floor sobbing intensely and having self-doubt. I had my very own private pity party. Still, in those moments there was a still small voice telling me to get back to work.

The next day at work, I learned that our building had flooded, and we were going to close, which meant I wouldn't have any funds coming in. I was devastated, and I couldn't go on with finishing my book. I reached out to my good friend Tasha, and she encouraged me to keep going, and that God would provide. Once again, I found myself rising within resilience. I labored day and night to complete my book, only to get in a car accident the day before my book signing. Satan was really throwing everything he could to hinder my progress. The emergency room was cold, and I was anxious to get out of there. I waited patiently for my test results. I was bored out of my mind. I'm actually in the *hospital the day before my book signing?* There was so much that I needed to do to prepare for the next day. I began to share my experience online on a social media site. I was hoping for some encouragement. I needed to read some words of kindness. As I began to scroll, I noticed a comment that was very wicked and extremely cruel. It was a demonic person trying to curse my future. I rebuked it in the name of Jesus Christ.

After a good night's rest, my body was sore, my legs and hips were hurting, and I was walking with a limp. I opened the door to my home church and waited for my makeup artist to paint my face. Everything in me was mentally drained. I had to put on a plastic smile and pretend by playing the part. My guests began arriving, and my sisters were ready to serve. God knew I needed my spirit lifted. He was always on time in my life. It was show time, I walked slowly into the café to greet my guests. I tried my best to disguise my limp. No one knew what I was going through. I noticed my mentor Lou who had travelled from Houston to support me. I looked to my left, and one of my dearest friends was making her way to the microphone. Tatiana 'Lady May' Mayfield was blessing the mic with a song by BeBe Winans, *We Found Love.* As she began to sing, my heart started to smile, and her voice was so uplifting.

Tatiana made my special day so memorable. She has a gift that is very rare, and I wanted her to share in my day. Tatiana and I met some years back at a Mother's Day brunch. When she graced the stage and began to sing, I was amazed at her vocals. I knew I wanted to meet the lady behind that beautiful voice. My name was called to recite a poem as a tribute to the mothers. At the conclusion of the brunch, I went over to introduce myself. It was intriguing how we were so complementary of one another. Her gift was incredibly beautiful, and in that moment, we supported each other. I got lost in her performance at my book signing. I knew everything was going to be okay.

I was exhausted and managed to embrace everyone at my all-white book-signing. God saw me through another test and trial. I conquered my goal of publishing my second book. I was extremely proud of the publication of this book. When you want to do good, evil is always present. I was in a good place when I got word that I was being looked down upon for having my book signing at the church café. I was so heartbroken; I didn't realize that it was such a major deal to have a small book signing. I didn't let that discourage me to leave my church. I took it, dusted my heart off again, and remained focused. God was truly grooming me to withstand and stay planted.

My heart became so full after serving God's people. I knew there was more in store for me to do. I had my heart set on empowering young people. God gave me a burden to assist ladies who had gone through major setbacks. I was blessed with an opportunity to speak at a detention center. My sister friends and I took a small road trip out of town. I was thinking about how God was going to lead me with my message. As we approached the juvenile center, I gathered my thoughts into a prayer. The ladies and I walked in with hopes of delivering a powerful message. I remember how rebellious I was as a young person, and I wanted to give back. As we walked onto the stage, I was examining the body language of the teens. Their bodies were saying, "I don't care what these ladies are about to say." Many of them had their arms folded, and I could have sworn, eyes were rolling. I wasn't scared! I was ready to change that negative energy.

I heard my name announced and I made my way to the microphone. I'm not sure what came over me. I talked about how I became a woman of resilience and before I knew it, I had their attention. I spoke about my experiences of growing up in a single parent home. They couldn't believe the mischief I shared with them. I was out in the streets doing ungodly things. Right away, they were intrigued, and they appeared very thirsty for more of my story. I couldn't wait to hear back from each person with whom I shared my story. My heart was soaring as I poured into their lives. I wanted them to know that they could overcome their mistakes. My objective was to empower them to see past their behavior. I was told so many things as a young person, and those words had power over me. I saw a bit of myself in those kids as they sat back in their chairs. They looked attentively at me and their body language changed.

I finished speaking and had a Q&A session with them. The anxiousness in the room was intense. I saw so many hands raised, and I wanted to answer everyone. A few of them wanted to know how I got past fatherlessness. I knew the Holy Spirit was going to take over. The anointing was purging the hearts in the room. I never dreamt that I could speak with such power. My voice was so weak and extremely faint at one period. God was planting my feet in a new era of purpose after that experience. I was captivated by speaking and wanted to do more.

I was silent for so long, and now I had the ability to change lives. God was listening to me, and He was ushering me to a new thing. That's it, God was doing a new thing! He was uniting my voice with His spirit to deliver and destroy brokenness. I was being raised up to overcome and conquer. The Lord was preparing me for His glory. There was oil and anointing churning and brewing in my spirit. The pain that I had overcome was set up to work for my good. I was destined to do great work in the lives of humanity.

While I was embracing being a true servant of Christ, I suffered pain in the process. There was always a need, and I wanted to fill it.

I served gracefully under the call of leadership. There was a huge calling on my life, and I didn't want to let God down. During the beginning of Sisters with Stories, I was being tested at every hand. I wanted to pray and serve humanity. As God ordered me, I followed His plan for my life. My sisters and I joined together to feed the homeless and honor single mothers. I have a huge heart for children and survivors of sexual assault. One evening, I got a call that one of my sisters had been diagnosed with cancer. I was devastated, and I wanted to gather the ladies together to help her. God gave me the green light, so I planned a Pink Purpose Party to lift her spirits. I asked those within our sisterhood if they would like to assist. We delegated tasks to each lady. It was so beautiful, the way the ladies loved on her. The sisters prepared meals to help her family.

We joined together for a prayer gathering as we believed Jesus for her healing. The ladies and I received donations to help with her financial needs. We made frequent visits to the hospital. I was so hopeful, and I knew that God was going to meet her at the point of her need. The lady who was carrying the weight of cancer was also a biological relative of mine. My family and I were trusting in the Lord for her healing. God is an Almighty God, and He saw her through her illness. I knew God was able! I saw the hand of God in a greater light, it made me believe in Him even more. My sisters and I were giving God the glory for healing her body. After a few months, I was elated to find out that she was ready to get back to serving.

We labored together to host a movie day for kids living in the homeless shelter. Everything was lovely, and I allowed her to take the lead to host the outreach event. The ladies of Sisters with Stories had opportunities to host events out in our community. I wanted to plant a seed of service in them. The overseer of the event was having trouble locating a projector for the movie day. I wasn't aware of it until I read about it on a social media site. I reached out to her and asked if she needed help. The shelter staff were so happy to have us come out. I was the first one to arrive, and the overseer of the event wasn't there. I waited out in the lobby until everyone arrived. The clock was ticking, and there was no sign of my cousin. I signed in at the front desk and decided to go out to the parking lot.

I saw her pull into the parking lot with a few people in her car. Everyone got out of the car, and I didn't recognize any of the ladies. I helped with gathering the items out of the car, and we went inside. As we prepared to set up, I noticed my Sisters with Stories' t-shirts. The ladies wore my t-shirts and I didn't know them. I thought that was odd, and I went over to introduce myself. "Hello, I'm the founder of Sisters with Stories, I'm Jocelyn."

They served with my ladies and the movie day was great. The kids enjoyed themselves. The children had a carnival snack bar and watched a Disney Film. The kids fell in love with my sisters. I noticed one of my sisters, crying and I asked her if she was ok. She mentioned that she grew up in a shelter as a young person. She was grateful for the opportunity to give back. We had a meeting later that week to discuss proper protocol. The ladies and I joined the conference call. I thanked everyone for coming out to support the movie day with the kids. I shared with them, "If there is ever a need for an event, please feel free to contact me."

My cousin wasn't pleased, and she was offended, but hid it very well. She became distant, and shortly after, she stopped communicating with me. I was devastated! I tried reaching out to her, but she refused to discuss what was bothering her. I wanted to lay in my hurt and forfeit my calling. Nevertheless, I didn't! I rose up once again, and I CONQUERED!

"And I will restore to you the years that the locusts hath eaten, the cankerworm, and the caterpillar, and the palmerworm, my great army which I sent among you." And ye shall eat in plenty, and be satisfied, and praise the name of the Lord your God, that hath dealt wondrously with you: and my people shall never be ashamed."

Joel 2:25-26

CHAPTER 11

Favored

Do what you can; God will do what you can't.

After I cried a river and wallowed in my sorrow, I managed to press past it all. God was showing me that I could handle the call on my life. He was equipping me throughout the process. I was being faithful by fulfilling the purpose orchestrated in His will. I was angry, but I wanted to push beyond it all. God was giving me vision for a few assignments. I felt an urgency in my spirit to help a single mother and her family. Christmas was approaching and I was in search for a family in need. I didn't know how I was going to make it happen with my budget. Jesus spoke to me, and I decided to look to social media for help. I began sending tweets and emails to local public figures in my area. I connected with two former NFL football players and a local Dallas news reporter to help. Sisters with Stories was being favored, and I was amazed by their response.

Can you believe that I had two things brewing in my spirit at the same time? One of them, I wasn't aware of. God had a way of showing me that I could produce multiple things. The Sisters with Stories team joined in with the efforts, and we received toys and clothing. At the conclusion of finalizing the details, I received a message from a man named Robbie. This gentleman said that he wanted to support me by giving to the family in need. I was so nervous and happy all at the same time. My emotions were dancing, and I was hesitant to reply to him. I did a little digging to see if we had mutual friends on Facebook. He lived in Indiana, and I didn't know him personally. Robbie told me he was going to drive to Texas to give the gifts himself. I was cautious when we initially spoke.

This man was contacting me constantly. He followed up with me a few days later, asking about hotels in the Dallas / Fort Worth area. He was serious! I had my suspicions, so I contacted someone who was connected to him. Robbie and I had a mutual friend named Tiffany. She said that he was an honest and upright guy. Tiffany assured me that he was genuine, and he did a lot of outreach. I was extremely happy to hear that he was an upright person. God was showing Himself to be true once again in my life.

I shared the news with my dad that following Sunday. I rushed into his office to tell him about my outreach assignment. Right away, I explained to him that a perfect stranger was driving in from Indiana. Now, to tell the truth, he did ask if I'd obtained a reference about him. I said yes! I told him that I got a reference from someone that I knew personally. Dad looked at me and said, "Daughter," as he handed me a check, "You are truly favored by God." I was so grateful for his donation to the family. In that moment, those words resonated with me. I didn't know what was ahead of me, but I was willing, and I was ready. The following week was hectic, because the donations came flooding in for the family. Robbie called to let me know that his friend couldn't make the trip with him. I was concerned, and I wanted him to make it safely. This man drove sixteen hours to help a family for the holidays. I called him as he drove to help with keeping him alert. Glory to God he made it safe and sound to Fort Worth!

The day of the surprise had finally arrived. My sisters and I loaded a few cars with the presents. Robbie met us at the home of the family, and it was time to surprise the kids. A homeless gentleman asked if he could assist us. My heart was smiling as I embraced what God was doing. We all grabbed the presents, as we walked to the front door. The mother was smiling as she welcomed us into her home. She made dessert and had beverages for us to drink. I thought, *how sweet was that to think of us in her time of need?* We went inside, and met the children. There were two boys and a little girl. I introduced myself and everyone in the room. The family sat down and began opening a few gifts with Robbie. The ladies joined him, and out of nowhere, I heard a loud scream. The kids were jumping around, as they opened up a gift. The mom was hugging her kids, and she and the little boys began to cry. The family said they were praying for a game station for Christmas. Robbie brought it down with him from Indiana. He mentioned to them that an eleven-year-old boy named Xavier wanted to bless them with his game station. Xavier told his mom that he overheard her conversation about the family's needs. He said that God placed it on his heart to give away his game station and his games. Everyone in the room was in tears. There wasn't a dry eye in the room. I was elated at God's goodness.

God heard those kids' prayer and put it on another child's heart to bless them. How beautiful is that? All I did was ask, and the provision was given to the family. I was blessed with a great gift, and it was to see this family overjoyed in that moment. Robbie brought clothing, toys and shoes for the family. He even stayed with the family after we said our goodbyes. You'd think I'd rest after something that took so much out of me. However, instead I reached out to a few local celebrities and began planning part two of my surprise for this family. I entitled it the 'Catch Dreams Tour.' I didn't know which way the vision would manifest. The family was blessed for Christmas, and they were so elated and overjoyed. I remember the little kids mentioning that they loved football. There were a few people I had in mind to help me pull this off. I knew exactly who would be perfect for the surprise. One of the gentlemen played for the Dallas Cowboys, and the other played for the Washington Redskins. I went on Twitter, to pitch my request to one of them. I explained to him that I wanted to host a Catch Dreams Tour at the Dallas Cowboys Stadium. He sent me his email address and the rest was history. I remember growing up witnessing struggle and sacrifice. Even at that time in my life, I was still discovering who I would become. I wanted to display some success stories in the presence of the kids. I needed something more, though—something that would make a greater impact.

Right away, I thought of a news reporter, by the name of Rebecca Lopez of Channel 8 News. I thought she'd be a perfect fit for the tour. I emailed Rebecca, and she gratefully accepted my invitation. My team and I gathered sports gear and Bibles to give out to the children. At the conclusion of our hard work, I was asked if I wanted a motivational speaker to join us. My God, I was overwhelmed with gratitude. My sisters invited more kids to join us on the Catch Dreams Tour. It was more than I had hoped for!

The next morning, we arrived at the Dallas Cowboys Stadium, and the former NFL players entered the building, and the kids' eyes lit up. Rebecca arrived as well, and I heard the whispers: "Hey, that's the lady from the news!" In that moment, my purpose was aligned to God's will. Jesse Holley and I led the tour and he explained to the children the strategies of the game. The kids got the opportunity to see the locker rooms and they played on the Dallas Cowboys field. The men joined in as they threw passes to the young people. At the end of the tour, we sat for an empowerment session with the kids They all looked so nice in their Catch Dreams Tour t-shirts. As they sat intently, I couldn't help but wonder, *what was going on in those young minds?* I was hoping that the experience was going to leave a positive mark within their hearts. I prayed that as they got older, they'd remember me. Childhood is so significant, positive empowering memories should be a part of it.

I wanted to erase terror from my own past by creating light in the lives of others. I smiled from the depths of my soul after that tour! My misery was finally working for my good. There I stood, in the midst of humanity, making my mark. I was becoming a living witness to resilience. I served God while I was serving His people. I realized God was onto something big for my life. After fighting for so long, I found myself in the same posture. I was fighting to be heard in a greater light. I was being favored, but was I really? Serving in God's kingdom was wonderful, but I wanted my story to be truly heard. I knew one day the masses would learn about my betrayal and torment. After being silent for so long, I wanted to tell the nation of how God brought me out. I felt like God let me down and so much was taken from me. I had dreams of becoming a wife and mother. I was getting much older, way beyond the childbearing age. I had to embrace the agony of it all.

I'm looking forward to the restored years that were stolen from me. The locust and cankerworm had its way in my life. To keep my sanity, I reminded myself that God removed me from the trauma and the night terrors. I didn't die in the hands of my live-in rapist. I didn't bleed to death vaginally as a young child. Glory be unto God! The triggers faded away after some time, but I continued to fight. I fought for victims of abuse. I took the hits; I endured the devastation and I stayed planted. I was crazy enough to believe that I was going to be on national television.

I contacted major Christian networks about my story, and they weren't interested. On one occasion, I was told that my story wasn't needed, and those words cut deeply. In my eyes, the network was agreeing with the predator. I was blown away, and couldn't fathom why they wouldn't accept me on their network. People are dying in their silence; kids are getting abused each day. I was outraged and it felt like salt was being poured in my wounds.

I was serving while in pain as I kept myself occupied. During the winter, I was feeding and clothing the homeless community. I would take on huge projects back to back. I was going non-stop, and I was making footprints in my purpose. God was using me to do greater things, and it was an honor to do just that. During my free time, I would look through magazines and read articles. I'd jump from my bed and grab a brush and read them aloud. "Hello, I'm Jocelyn Ja'Net, and I'm coming to you live from Dallas, Texas." I was training my voice, even though I didn't realize it at the time. We as a people must believe, even though the blessing is not visible. I was operating in faith. I was getting to know another dream that was within me. I'd watch Entertainment Tonight and dream of interviewing celebrities. I saw a beautiful woman on the show who reminded me, that I could do it too. God was listening to my heart in that moment. I was in preparation and didn't know it at the time.

My steps were being ordered, and I didn't realize it. I was introduced to a lady named Ashton, who had a start-up magazine, and she was seeking a media intern. As soon as we met, things quickly took off. I didn't know exactly what she was looking for, but she did. I met Ashton in downtown Dallas one evening for a video shoot. When I arrived, I noticed that there were other ladies waiting with her. Everyone was so friendly, and we began recording a video for her magazine. I was so happy for the opportunity to share in her vision. Ashton got all the footage she needed, and we completed the goal for the day. Over the next few days, I was waiting to hear back from her. I later received a call from Ashton, asking if I wanted to attend a networking event. I gladly accepted the invitation, and we were in route to the hotel. I met the overseer of the event and a few cameramen. I was so captivated by the ambience of the hotel. Everything was delightful, and I knew we were going to have a fabulous night. Ashton came over to tell me that I was going to interview the guests at the party. I was stunned! She kind of sprung it on me, and I was in shock, asking tons of questions. I've never interviewed anyone, other than when I practiced in my mirror. Then something dawned on me; I was just saying to God how I wished I had applied for school. Broadcasting and journalism would have been my choice. There wasn't any time for me to panic, because it was time to start the interview.

There I was, standing on the red carpet, and Ashton handed me the microphone. My nerves took a seat, and something came over me. I was introducing her magazine and myself to the camera. When the lights flashed, I was embodying the role of an entertainment reporter. It felt like I was having a conversation with the guests. I laughed and smiled, tossed my hair, and I was symbolizing the moment. At the end of the night, I was on such a high and couldn't get any sleep. I was reliving what I had just experienced, and my mind was racing. I thought to myself, *what did I just do?* After my experience at the hotel I was offered the media host position for Ashton's magazine. Well, of course, I accepted, and things just kind of took off. We were getting a few gigs in the Dallas / Fort Worth area. The line-up of people I was interviewing were models, businessmen, actors, and ministry leaders. I was building my resume, and people were beginning to take notice. I was getting tagged on social media with comments like, "Hey, that's the lady who interviewed me!" I was starting to feel like my favorite correspondent, Shaun Roberson. When I'd heard the word *"favored"* time and time again in church, I began to embrace it. God was literally putting me in the pathway of greatness. I was flourishing within my gifts. By this time, I had my hand in a few things.

I was wearing many hats, and I didn't mind. My ministry was evolving, and I was planting my feet in the community. Sisters with Stories had reached a few milestones. We conquered one year of service. The beginning was tough for me, but I pressed through it. I was discovering me. God was encouraging me to use the gifts that I had in my hand. He was showing me my capacity! Jesus was showing me my capabilities. He was proving all my doubters wrong.

Even in the midst of discovering my gifts, I was trying to figure out how to profit from them financially. The reward of gratitude was enough, but I had financial needs to fulfill. I was honored to be used by God in various ways. Many nights, I pleaded with God on my behalf. I asked Him to open a door for me to walk through. I needed God to give me prestige. My dream was to travel the world and make a difference. I didn't know how to execute what I was feeling. I had a vision, and I needed God to fund what was planted in me. The Bible tells us if we seek ye first the kingdom of God, and its righteousness, all things shall be added unto us. I was at one of the lowest lows in my life when I began doubting my abilities. Discouragement was taking root, and I was having a huge pity party. I laid out in the floor as I held my second book in my arms. Tears began streaming down my face. I was beginning to believe that I wouldn't be successful, nor would I find love.

As I laid helplessly on the floor, I reached over for my cell phone. I logged onto social media, and I began watching a video. As I watched the clip, it began to minister to my spirit. God was using DeVon Franklin and Meagan Good to bless me through their message. The message was very intriguing, and my spirit began to lift as they spoke about finding love. I wiped my tears, got up off the floor, and got my act together. The next day as I was leaving work, my phone rang, and it was Ashton telling me that she had exciting news.

She and I met up for a brief meeting, and she began smiling from ear to ear. I was like, "Girl, spill the news already!" She mentioned to me that she and I, along with her team, were invited to a charity gala. She said that we were going to attend a private cocktail hour before the festivities. I was happy, but I was so anxious to hear more. She sent me an email that stated who would be in attendance. The email read the names of the following people: DeVon Franklin, Meagan Good, Keshia Knight Pulliam, and Emmitt Smith, just to name a few. I literally felt faint! Anxiety was surfacing, and I shouted, "O-M-G! My God!" I was just watching them speak the other day! She looked me in the eyes, reassuring me that I could do this. My brief tenure of doing correspondent work was so new to me. I was an amateur when it came to interviewing celebrities. There were a thousand things running through my mind. What in the world was I going to ask them? What was I going to wear?

This was such a huge opportunity, and I didn't want to fall on my face. Things were happening so fast, and my nerves had to be pushed aside. I had to prepare. I went through the list of the names, and I researched the charity. My evening consisted of finding the right outfit and hairstyle, and I couldn't forget about accessories. I had so much that was against me as I prepared for the gala. As the week progressed, I continued to push forward with the assignment that was before me. I didn't know what to expect when Ashton and I arrived at the gala. We had to prepare for makeup before the red-carpet interviews. I mentioned to Ashton that I wanted to meet Whitney Houston's family. Whitney had passed away prior to this gala. I told her that I wanted to feel Whitney's presence through her family. Now, let me say this: God was listening. We made it to the room where women were getting their face painted. We waited for our turn to get our makeup done, and in walks a fashion stylist, none other than the legendary Mr. J Bolin himself from Mississippi. I nearly fainted when I looked to my right, and he was styling a lady with his gifted hands. I love his work and made sure he knew it. I asked him for his business card, and he mentioned that he didn't have one on him. We exchanged numbers. You know, those small nuggets from God I've been mentioning? Well, that was one of them! The room was full of influential people. I sat quietly for a moment as I thought, *how did I qualify to be among these greats?*

I'm thinking it was my gift making room for me. To the right, I saw NFL wives, Oprah Winfrey's colleagues, and outreach leaders. As I lavished in the moment, I couldn't think of anything, but your gift will make room for you and present you before the great. I heard the door open, and in walks Patricia Houston. She was the sister-in-law of Whitney Houston. I stood up as if Whitney herself walked in with her. As she walked towards me, I reached out my hand to introduce myself. Pat opened her arms to give me a hug, and we embraced. As I held her, I was so overwhelmed at the awesomeness of God. She was so kind and affectionate, and I did get what I asked for. There was a warmth of dear Whitney Elizabeth Houston within that embrace. Everything was happening so fast, and we were making our way down the hallway. It was show time.

I walked into a huge room with bright lights, the red carpet, and the Entertainment Tonight backdrop. Yes, Entertainment Tonight. I was looking in every direction as I noticed the stars all around me. It felt like Hollywood was sitting in Texas. I was honored to be there to celebrate such a worthy charity. There were so many people in attendance, and I didn't know who I was going to interview. Ironically, the very first person I interviewed was from the Bay Area. She was standing on the red carpet in a bright red dress, and her hair was flawless. She was very beautiful. Her name was Brely Evans—actress, producer, singer, and model.

I was so nervous, but as soon as I felt her energy, my nerves subsided. Talking with Brely was like having a conversation with a sister friend. She was so funny, and her light was beaming. I was so thankful for her in that moment, because she helped ease my nerves. I knew she wouldn't be the only one that I would interview, so I was ready.

Next up was Keshia Knight Pulliam, from *The Cosby Show*. I was so thrilled to speak with her. I had grown up watching her on the show. She was such a nice person, and I couldn't wait to ask her about the camp she founded. I had to ask her about giving back and supporting worthy causes. Keshiha wore a sleek black gown, and she was extremely radiant On the inside, I was saying 'Rudy,' but of course, I never called her that.

The third person that I interviewed was none other than NFL great Emmitt Smith. I was snapping a few photos when someone tapped me on the shoulder and said, "Emmitt's ready for the interview." I took a deep breath and walked over to him with as much confidence as I could possess. I greeted him, and shortly after the cameras began rolling. I remember exactly how I was feeling in that moment. It was pure gratefulness. There I was, standing next to the great, living legend, Emmitt Smith. After the interview, Emmitt said to me, "Keep up the good work." I was so proud. God was confirming, once again, that I was worthy. My heart was so full, and I was more than ready for my next interview.

As I waited for the next person to arrive for their interview, I noticed Meagan and DeVon walking nearby, and I walked over to say hello. They were so kind and down to earth.

Just standing in their presence made me appreciate our Savior even more. Meagan is of my favorite actresses, and DeVon has an amazing success story and he's from the Bay Area. Two people from the Bay Area in one night. This kid who grew up in the Bay Area, is destined to prosper. My heart was smiling! The Franklin's wrote a book together, and they saved themselves until marriage. I was smitten. If I ever needed anyone in that moment, it would be God to hold my hand, because I couldn't believe all that I was seeing. I was pulled away to be introduced to Kirk and Tammy Franklin. No introduction needed! Kirk and I are both are from Fort Worth—how amazing is that? Kirk made a few jokes about me being tall, and I was smiling, staring down at him.

My night ended with some drama with Ashton, but I didn't let her negativity steal my joy. I knew God was up to something, and I was not going to let anyone stand in my way. Days went by, and I hadn't heard anything from Ashton. She was such an emotional person at times. I needed my space and I had to reflect on that amazing night. God was showing me, even in His time of blessings, evil can be present itself. I'm not saying she was evil, but she was being used by it. She ended up moving away, and I wasn't hurt or bothered by it.

Behold, the righteous shall be recompensed in the earth: much more the wicked and the sinner.

Proverbs 11:31

CHAPTER 12

Restitution

Multiple Streams of Wealth.

I've always loved cosmetics. I wanted to learn more about artistry, and I was hungry. I began seeking God about my purpose, but why was He holding back? There were many nights where I wondered if God was listening to me. My eyes were so focused on how He was opening doors for other people. In my mind, I thought, what about the little girl who laid helplessly in bed while she was raped on a consistent basis? God, what are You doing? Where is my restitution? After I sobbed tearfully, my anger always conquered my spirit. The sun would set, and the moon rose to embrace the night. As usual, I'd get lost in my worship as well as my gifts.

While I was in school, I fell head over heels for makeup application. I practiced on family members and friends. If I wanted something, I wasn't afraid of going after it. I needed to learn more about my craft. I worked so hard to hustle my way to get to New

York City to invest in my craft. Each and every time I tried to evolve in something, guess who was waiting, trying to stop me? I couldn't stand the mere idea of Satan himself. I was so blessed to earn the funds for my tuition for my class. I couldn't believe that I was going to New York. Truthfully, I was being groomed to increase my abilities and my confidence. God used my mentors, Mr. Posley and Mr. Crimson, to ignite my desire and help my disbelief. When I was painting my model in New York City, my educator and mentor gave me a compliment. He told me that I was really great with skin. He also told me that when I paint, I am painting a story. His light was so bright, and I wanted to rest in it.

He said that he always wanted to stand upon his story, and not in it. His words were so profound, and they are sketched in my heart forever. I remember following his work and admiring his skill of artistry through social media. I admired the way he held his brush and worked with so much passion. I would get lost in his videos and say to myself, "One day, I'm going to learn from him." We met in Dallas, and I remember looking to my right, and there he was. I walked over and introduced myself. I asked if I could give him a hug, and he gladly accepted. His energy was such a delight as he began sharing his soothing yet warm words with me. He told me that he loved what I was doing with Sisters with Stories. I was curious to know more about his artistry, but he was encouraging me not to give up on Sisters with Stories.

As he shared his heart, I began to cry. I was tearful because his light was so moving. When you meet a soul as beautiful as his, it's truly a gift from God. After I wiped my tears, I told him that I'd one day train with him in New York. Guess what? I did! Fast forward to the realization of that prophecy spoken. There was opposition at the hotel and right up until my class, I almost cancelled it. I pushed past being exhausted and I met up with Mr. Posley. I prayed, and my friend encouraged me to continue. I arrived at the studio, and when I saw him, my mood completely shifted when I heard his voice. His voice was so calming. After my class, I had my heart set on building my kit and my clientele.

Unfortunately, I was having feelings of weakness, and a few other symptoms that had me down. During that entire year, all I could think about was painting. I remember ailing upon my bed, and I dreamt of painting some very beautiful, expensive skin looks. After multiple tests and visits to the emergency room, I was diagnosed with an illness that the doctors said was incurable. I was devastated, and my dream of becoming a great makeup artist had drifted beyond the clouds. I didn't want to do anything. But God had other plans. A well-known, black owned businessman managed to contact me. I was so empowered to keep going. Mr. Crimson was another artist I was following, and his work spoke for itself. Before I was diagnosed with my illness, I purchased a ticket to the Beauty for Brunch event. The event was approaching, and I seriously didn't want to attend, because I was totally devastated. I arrived at the venue and I waited in the lobby. Mr. Crimson came to greet his guests before the event started. He walked up to us with his beautiful smile and his astonishing ray of light. We greeted one another, and we went to the venue area. I walked to the end of the table to sit in the back. I was still in a funk from my diagnosis and I wanted to stay in my bubble. I was there but I had given up on becoming a makeup artist. As I walked towards my chair, I heard, "Jocelyn! Your seat is right here." Crimson had my name at the head of the table, right alongside him. I was so baffled, and I couldn't say no.

After all, he was one of the men I admired in the industry. This was the man who I had followed for years and the reason why I attended multiple workshops and pro-on-the-go classes. He was so amazing. He wasn't arrogant, he was extremely humble, and I adored him. I recall a time when he traveled to Africa, handling major business deals for his makeup line AJ CRIMSON Beauty. He encouraged me to believe in my ability. He could have easily ignored my messages when I would reach out. He complimented my work before I had any training, so to see him stand at the head of the Beauty Brunch table and asked me to sit right beside him meant the world to me. He didn't know it, but that was God using him to empower me to keep walking. I'll always love and appreciate him for his light, and artistry. My gifts were still attempting to make room for me. My diagnosis has been a struggle and had gotten the best of me. Most days, I was extremely fatigued and saddened. The only thing that I could find comfort in was knowing that God was going to heal me. One morning while I was looking for my medication, God spoke and said, "Daughter, I'm going to heal you." His words were so piercing to my soul, and I couldn't do anything but say, "Thank you." My heart is fixed upon what He said He's going to do! As I continued to share my story, I would keep my vision at the forefront. I saw a post on the page of none other than Meagan Good's Instagram. She, along with her sister, shared my story on their platform.

I was stunned when I read my direct message. *'Out of thousands of followers who follow them, they chose my story?'* There goes God sharing another one of those little nuggets of favor. They asked their supporters to share a snippet of why they should be chosen for the giveaway. I received a Defend Good Girl shirt. I'm so thankful that God used the Good sisters to bless me. I was amazed to see my picture posted on Meagan and Lamyia's Instagram page. God was positioning my steps. I remember talking with my aunt and my friend Laura about the recurrences I had with celebrities. I was working in a field that I had outgrown and there I was, connecting with greatness. I asked Laura, "I wonder why God keeps putting me in the pathway of stars?" My Auntie Evelyn would always say, "Because you are going to be working with them."

In my mind I couldn't receive what she had spoken. I was this poor kid from not one but two hoods. How in the world was I going to accomplish that? God is so unpredictable. The complete mysteries of God will reveal themselves in time. Time and time again, I'd get these prophetic revelations from people. God spoke on many occasions through a lot of prophets about my life. Once I became closer with God, He began speaking to me. My dear friend Katrice would hear right down from heaven. One Sunday morning, she said, "Jocelyn, I had a dream about you." Katrice said that she saw me standing on a large platform speaking to thousands of people.

A friend of my mother's told me the exact same thing. I didn't know what to do with this information other than trust the process. I wasn't aware that I needed to prepare for the promise to be revealed. God was pouring into me like never before and I had to get in position. I was well on my way toward receiving all that God had in store for me. I'd speak out into the atmosphere, "DeVon Franklin, you are going to produce my story." I then said the same thing about Tyler Perry and Bishop T.D. Jakes. I didn't know exactly who was going to do it, but I knew it would be done.

My dear friend Carla and I were having lunch one evening. She mentioned I would one day have my own talk show. I looked at her as I did the others, saying to myself, *well ok*. This went on for years, individuals pouring into my life. I believe a big part of me didn't believe it because so much time had gone by. It wasn't much, but I still had my mustard seed faith in my heart. God didn't let my lack of belief hinder what He was about to do in my life. I grabbed my cell and spoke that my story would one day be produced into a movie. There were a few people who wanted to use my story. I had a gentleman who wanted to produce a short film about my life. I turned that offer down. After all that I had been through, I wanted something greater. A well-known local celebrity wanted to publish my story in her book. They sent me the contract stating all the details.

She offered me tickets to her book signing. I wouldn't receive royalties for my story being in her book. That was an insult and a slap in the face. I had a lawyer look over the contract before I responded to her assistant. I lost a great multitude because of a sick predator. My mind said, "Girl, they must be crazy!" If anyone was going to profit from my pain, I thought it should be me. I politely turned them down, and they wished me well on the publication of my future memoir. I knew then, that I wasn't star stuck! God was showing me how significant my story of redemption was to others.

After receiving crazy publishing deals, that left me in the dark, I pulled away from working on my book. I needed a break. Truthfully, it was years before I decided to give it a go. Thankfully, I met a lady by the name of Gwendolyn who spoke a word about my writing. God used her and her husband to release a timely word that ushered me to start writing again. I praise God for the call that is on their life. I spoke victory in my mind periodically, not knowing it was being produced in the spirit realm. God was listening to me and made me aware of it one Sunday. I was invited to church by Brother Omar and I pushed my way to attend. God was speaking through him and the word was building my spirit. During the conclusion of the service, Jesus spoke to me. My God, this was an experience that

I have never had before. This man of God walked up to me saying, "Jocelyn, it's not just books, but I see movies."

It hit the core of my soul and I did a hurdle over my mother and ran and collapsed on the floor of the church. He went on to say, "I see Hollywood." I was so overwhelmed by the first statement that I began speaking in my heavenly language. God told me so much, I had to process it all that following week. How in the world was I going to reside in Hollywood? I wasn't going to wrack my brain trying to figure it out. I recall DeVon Franklin saying, "the how is not our business, it's God's." My focus then began to shift, and I began listening to the consistency series by Toure Roberts, which ignited my soul. I had to play my hand with the gifts that were given to me. I was so thankful for the word that he carried.

God was setting bridges in my path at a crucial time in my life. It was a period that Christ was using these people to get me to the finish line of what you're reading right now. I began following my favorite gospel singer, Deitrick Haddon's church online. He said something so profound, "there is victory in consistency." God was aligning me with the word of God. I was learning to hear God's voice in a greater way. Pastor Haddon taught a series about locating God's voice. His voice was being amplified in my life. Each time an opportunity was centered around positivity, I'd support it by sharing my gifts. Can you believe that I got an opportunity to do freelance media interviews again? I was overwhelmed with joy. This was presented to me by an organization that help women in domestic violence situations. Every opportunity presented itself with some sort of battle. I had to prepare myself, because when God wanted to bless, evil was making its move. I became so familiar with the tactics that I stayed sober to the devices of the adversary. I hope that, through my experiences, you will find strength to press past yours.

Fast forward to the charity gala, where I was going to be the keynote interviewer. I chose to wear a cobalt blue dress. It was a long dress that hugged my physique. My finances weren't where I needed them to be, so I styled my own hair and painted my face. I was extremely grateful to God in those moments, I was putting my gifts to work. When I arrived at the venue, I couldn't help but admire the beautiful ambience. Everything was extravagant, and I met with the ladies working at the gala. I needed to know where I'd be working, and the guests who needed to be interviewed. I was a little rusty, and I hadn't worked the red carpet in a while. My sister friend Nikki reassured me that I'd do well. She always had a way of lifting me up in those moments. Lights, camera, action, and it was time to make my mark again. The line-up of guests consisted of lawyers, business owners, mayors, and a few millionaires. At the time, I didn't know everyone, but I did my very best. The night was phenomenal. I heard stories from domestic violence survivors, including the songbird herself, Michel'le.

I walked alongside an empty table where no one was sitting. There were picture frames that were placed on top of the tables. Each frame had a picture of a survivor who died from abuse. My heart sank as I looked at the eyes of each lady in those pictures. I was saddened, yet happy that I could give of myself to help fight against violence. As I thanked God for giving me a heart to serve, I rested peacefully that night. "God," I said, "You are an amazing Savior." When I looked back over my life, I began to recall moments where He truly saw me through. I was pulled out of so much horror to find my hands doing an even greater work. Serving became my normal and the opportunities didn't stop coming.

My sisters and I had the opportunity to speak at a Child Protective Services event. The day we were scheduled to speak was around Easter. The ladies and I met up at the location, and a few of them went in. When we arrived, I noticed the building looked familiar to me. Right away, memories of my past began to flood my mind. I got out of the car and walked to the door with my friend. I opened the door and I stood there. I was shocked, and I was stuck, and I literally couldn't move. My friend asked me what was wrong. I remember a cloud of darkness flooding right in front of me as I stood in the doorway. My body was weak, I felt like I was drowning, and my feet felt like they were standing in cement. I began taking deep breaths, trying to explain what was happening to me. "I can't go in there," I said. "I just can't go inside." This was the place I had to go as an eleven-year-old child.

My mind began reliving the moments of what happened in that building. The Child Protective Service issued a letter stating I had to meet with them. I was taken into a room and a lady came inside. She was holding baby dolls and asked me some questions. I thought we were going to play, seeing she had so many dolls in her hand. The lady asked me about the baby dolls and their body parts. I answered the questions to the best of my ability. My eleven-year-old mind didn't know why she was asking me all these questions. I just wanted to play with her. She pulled the dolls' clothing off and pointed to the private areas. She asked about the vagina and the penis. I was very quiet in that moment. I simply didn't know how to respond. She later asked if anyone touched me there with a penis, and I said yes. So, fast forward more than twenty plus years later, and I was now standing at that same building. I was having a panic attack, and I managed to walk away from the door. I went and I sat down to tell my friend what was happening to me. Anxiety was rising, and it had me to the point of not wanting to go in. I had to think quickly, so I called my dad, Bishop Young, but he didn't answer the phone. Next on my list was Auntie Evelyn. She said, "Now, you know you can walk through those doors, right?" I was so fearful and afraid to go inside of that building. It was like time had gone in reverse, and I was eleven again. I got off the phone with her and tried again.

I went up to the front door, but as soon as the doors opened, I turned around. "I can't do it!" I shouted. I was a wreck. My people were already inside and I had to walk away. I then called my brother, Christopher, and I told him everything. He began to encourage me by saying, "You can do this." I hung up the phone and walked back to the door. The phone buzzed again. It was my dad calling. He said, "Daughter, are you okay?" I told him what was going on, and he counseled me. His words were so short, but powerful. I hung up the phone and took all of them with me as I walked into the front doors of the building. My friend was there, and she held my hand. I took a step inside of the building. The noise I heard and darkness I was feeling vanished. I did it, I made it inside, and I shared my story alongside my sisters, the ladies of Sisters with Stories. It was powerful beyond measure.

After that day, I faced each day with platinum faith and courage. I'm such a creative, and I always find ways to create doors of opportunity. I managed to create an atmosphere for my audience of followers. My prayer line was growing by this time, and there was something I needed to do. I decided that I wanted to have another platform for people to share their stories. I searched for guests to be featured on my conference line. Deep down, I always wanted to place my hands in radio broadcasting. I asked locals to share their hearts on my weekly conference line. After a few weeks, I was amazed at the response from the interviews.

The line-up consisted of business owners, fashion stylists, ministers and world changers. I've interviewed celebrity chefs, make-up artists, and hair stylists. Many of them could identify with my past, and they were more than willing to join on my call. My interviews always started with prayer, and we'd follow up with a thirty-minute interview. God was truly using me to bless lives by using this platform. At the end of the call, we would give time for questions and answers. In those times, God was showing me that I was in alignment with His plan for my life.

I began working behind the scenes to prepare for my next interview. My next guest speaker was introduced to me by my cousin Edward. I was so anxious, and I didn't want him to hold out any longer. I couldn't believe the words that were coming out of his mouth. Two words, "Dave Hollister." Wait a minute, the legendary musical genius will grace my conference line? Humility always played a role within me, especially after God displayed blessings in my life. I was amazed each time I met up with greatness. God, you really know how to constantly show me my worth. There He goes again connecting me with influential people. Edward mentioned that he asked him to be a guest on my prayer line. I was grateful for the connection. My cousin, always looking out for my best interests. Right away, I began writing down an interview topic, and it was entitled, 'unbandage your wounds.' I wanted my callers to dial in and let themselves be vulnerable during the call.

I covered my wounds for so many years, and I was hiding my hurt. There were many others out there just like me, and they, too, were hurting. I was burying my hurt, because I was fearful of being judged. I didn't want anyone to know that I didn't have it all together. God had to pull back the bandages so that I could truly heal. I wanted the same for those who walked in my shoes. After I designed my flyer for the call, it began to sink in. I was astonished at how the Bible was coming alive in my life. It was hard to believe that my gifts were continuing to make room for me. I am such a lover of music, and music has been such a huge vehicle towards healing in my life. When I think about the power behind Deitrick Haddon's song, 'He's Able,' it has pulled me from many pits. Music has the capacity to cause you to clap your hands and lavish in the essence of entertainment. Music transcends, and it uplifts. There I was, sitting in front of my computer, staring at my newly designed flyer with Dave Hollister on it. I was a young person when I began listening and appreciating his music. His vocal ability is beyond description. When I hear him sing any genre of music, it's captivating. I truly wanted to understand why he sings with so much conviction. After he spoke so powerfully on my conference line, I got the answer to that question. The Lord was speaking through his soul. Pastor Hollister shared the word and it was piercing. God was present in that divine moment of transparency.

God was pushing me closer to His purpose and plan for my life. I was amazed at His power, but I was graciously humbled at His uncommon favor in my life. God was showing me in distinct ways that He was for me. Christ the Lord was allowing my gifts to make room for me by presenting me before great men. Jesus anointed His son and kept His mind to be sustained in perfect peace. God graced Dave Hollister to lead, heal and restore broken hearts through the Holy Spirit. There wasn't a force that could stop the destiny of this man of God. When I think back to each storm and word curse spoken over me, I smile because it didn't work. God really knows how to pull me to a place that I try to bury.

My cousin Tanicia asked me if I wanted to write a chapter in a book she was publishing. I was hesitant at the beginning, but I had to accept her offer. To tell you the truth, I couldn't comprehend why was I saying yes to her offer. In the midst of writing, I began to reflect on how far I had come. I went from the depths of sorrow to the rising of greater heights. God truly has a place in my journey of recovery. There is no way I could have made it to this very day, without Christ. God was my lifeline, and each time I wanted to take an eternal night's rest, God was there. When I was drowning in years of depression, He was there. I owe God my life, and I plan on doing just that. I booked a flight to Oakland, California to attend the Broken into Brilliance Conference. It was a great being honored inside such a holistic book.

As I sat at the airport, I thought about Zephaniah 3:19-20, "I will bring you again to all the places you suffered shame." I was heading home; I was flying back to the Bay Area. I, Jocelyn Ja'Net, was going to the very place where I had experienced an enormous amount of child sexual assault. I had shared my story publicly in Texas more than I could count. This was my first time speaking publicly in Pittsburg, California. How would I compile words to describe my life? It was time for me to conquer in my city. My introduction was announced, and I walked to the podium to speak. I began giving honor to God first, because it was an honorable thing to do. I followed with the beloved Maya Angelou and my spiritual dad, Bishop Richard E. Young. As my mouth began to form the words *'Pittsburg, California,'* I lost my speech and I began sobbing as tears fell from my eyes. I stood there, trying to fight the flooding of tears while trying to speak. I inhaled a bit as the words from my family encouraged me from afar.

Moments later, I gasped, and Jesus stood in that moment with me. I did it! I spoke for the first time in a place where Satan tried to destroy my very soul. Deep down, I believe my six-year old self was in the crowd cheering me on, saying, "You can do it, do it for me." You know what? I did it for her. I spoke brilliantly through my tears. God was smiling upon me.

That next morning, my family and I prepared for Sunday morning service. The break of morning was beautiful to me. My heart was at peace and joy was ringing in my soul. I walked inside of church with my Auntie Evelyn, and we chose our seats. This was my first time visiting her church. Pastor Hollister was speaking as we took our seat. We sang some good old-fashioned hymns and I enjoyed worship. I'm a worshipper at heart, so I was feeling wonderful. I was anxious to hear the word of God and I looked forward to meeting him. I recall telling him that I would visit his church. He noticed that I was sitting in the congregation. Now you know Pastors, they will give recognition to visitors. He was delightful as he introduced me to the congregation. It felt like God had given me a new name of valor and I was being reintroduced to the world. He went on to say, "Jocelyn has a powerful story." I was standing in Zephaniah 3:19, I was driven out and I was being praised in a land where I suffered shame. Thank you, Lord!

So, what's next for the little girl who lives on the inside of me? We'll just have to wait and see! Stay tuned for the fruition and the evolvement of me. God's redemptive power is real and I'm a living testament to that!

What Satan meant for evil, God turned it around for my good. Better is the end of a thing than its beginning. If I could preserve words in your heart it would read, be brave, be bold, be free. We overcame Satan by the blood of the Lamb and by the words of our testimony.

Revelations 12:11

Resiliently Restored,

Jocelyn Ja'Net Willis

I Overcame, and I Conquered

Acknowledgements

Thank you first and foremost to my Lord and Savior Jesus Christ. Since the beginning, You've been my rock, my peace in the storm and my lifeline. Before the foundation of the world, You placed me in Your plans. You were aware of each obstacle I would face. I was engrafted into Your hands because You knew they would always hold me up. Those same hands rescued me and put the pieces of my shattered heart together again. You rose again because You knew I'd need that same power to get up. Through it all, my heart has its beat and You're walking beside me on this journey. Thank you for not giving up on me! I love you with an ever-lasting love. My wonderful and amazing Savior, Jesus Christ.

I would like to recognize my family for supporting me through life lessons. Thank you for giving of yourself. Too many to name, I love you.

Mother, I am grateful to have you here to witness this accomplishment. I can't imagine raising children alone, but you did. You made choices in life that changed the trajectory of my life. I endured so much, that you can't comprehend the magnitude of my loss. I'm grateful that God does. I forgive you and your former husband for your actions. I pray that God restores you internally and completely. I love you, Mama.

Christopher Michael Willis, you were the first example of a consistent male figure in my life. You cared for me as a kid and drove me nuts as an adult. I appreciate you for your existence. It is my prayer that you discover our Savior in a greater depth. May God restore you from within from the pain of your past. I love you, Brother.

Grandma, you are witnessing this moment with me in spirit. You were the matriarch of our family. I am thankful for your love and nurture. I wish we had more time together. I love and miss you dearly.

Father, I thank you because I exist. Thank you for making the decisions that you made. I am the person that I am because of those choices. I forgave you a long time ago for your absence. God stepped in and carried me in this journey. Love you with God's love.

Nyah Marie, you will always be my pretty princess. You are such a beautiful light. Your ability to evolve in your gifts is beyond amazing. I pray that you'll reach every dream and live life to the fullest. May Christ watch over you every step of the way. I love you.

Bishop Richard E. Young, I want to thank you for being there for me as I journeyed out of my teens, until now. I can't believe it's been twenty-one years. You were following your calling the year I was born. God was getting you prepared to not only minister, but to father, the fatherless. Ironically, I fell victim to abuse from my mother's ex-husband around the time you began pastoring. Christ used you to get me to a place of liberty. God had you lined up to cross pathways with me. Thank you for the numerous affirmations that led me past the rejection that haunted me. You knew I'd be free from the terror of my past and my heartbreak. Dad, you believed I would love again. Thank you for hurting when I hurt and wanting the best for me. Thank you for expecting greatness from me. I love you to life! God bless you and Lady Arlene for your dedication and love.

Bishop Marvin Sapp, your gift of song is a lifeline to humanity. My testimony lyrics truly rest upon my heart. As I rose beyond the ashes of my past, your music was a vehicle of transportation towards healing. Thank you for accepting the call of leadership of The Chosen Vessel Cathedral Church. God Bless.

Dr. Zack and Apostle Gwendolyn Ponyo, you are a powerful couple in the kingdom. I bless God for you both. Thank you for your obedience to the call. God has a great abundance of favor that will overshadow Kingdom for All Nations. I speak blessings over you. Your inclined ears to God ignited me to write my book. I'm grateful for the word that lives within you. Love you!

Auntie Evelyn, I give you my heart of gratitude. You are a significant part of my journey. Thank you for being my shield as a child. You covered me in prayer and supported my ministry. I appreciate you for igniting me to believe in my purpose. I love you.

Fingers, Fats, Tina, Tyree, Marie, Tanicia, Corinne, Cassius, Grant, Vanessa, my girls, Nefertari, Tamara and Phylethia. Thank you all for being the calm and laughter in my childhood. I love you.

Edward Mathis, I want you to know that your tears aren't forgotten, they will exceed your expectation. God will use you for His glory like never before. We've embraced many storms but just know they will work for your good. I love you beyond measure.

Dr. Dave Hollister, thank you for speaking God's truth over my life. It meant a lot to have you cover the people on my conference line. God has great things in store for you and the Church 4 Me family. Blessings to you and Lady Ayana. Thank you for giving us great music. Keep schooling them newbies, bro! You are a musical genius! I love you.

Bishop T.D. Jakes, "Forever the Victim, I Don't Think So." This sermon pulled me from a low place at a crucial and distinct time in my life. I was resurrected from a mentality of victimization. The lower I went was an indication of how high I would go. You blew wind to my understanding with these words! I salute you for your obedience to the call. I am the comeback kid who is ready for divine immigration! Bless You, Bishop T.D. and First Lady Serita Jakes, & Cora Jakes Coleman!

Pastor Deitrick Haddon, thank you for your resurrecting anointing. Your music has been a lifeline in my journey towards healing. There were many days, I was slipping into a deep depression, and the Holy Ghost power within your music brought me back. Thank you for never giving up, because you are needed. I appreciate you for covering me in prayer. I concur, they are coming from the north, south, east, and west. Watch out Hill City Church Los Angeles. God bless you and First Lady Dominique Haddon & the kids.

Toure "PT" & Sarah Jakes Roberts, I've followed your teachings and they have propelled me towards the completion of this book. I'm tremendously grateful for the power behind your ministry. Your union alone, has caused the masses to believe in identifying their soulmates. I'm ready to eat like a king. I am evolving in consistency, while playing my hand! The Bow, The Arrow & the Promise.

Aunt Laura Johnson, I believe that your spirit is still with our family. Your willingness to impart prayer in my life was one of the best gifts you've ever given. I'll always cherish you for that. Your love and dedication spoke volumes. Those same prayers you prayed are still covering our family immensely.

Thank you, Felicia Guimont, Rodrick Conner, Belinda Carter, Quintarus Carter, Danielle Hall, Winnie Starks and Josie Castro. I appreciate you for pouring words of light into my life. May God bless you richly.

Thank you, Eric B. Ramsey and Shannon Thomas for your contribution to my book. God bless you.

Nicky Posley and AJ Crimson, I have a great depth of gratitude for you guys. Your very purpose ushered me towards discovering my love for artistry in a greater way. My confidence grew because of your kindness and encouragement. Thank you for your light.

You all keep my faith alive with your friendship. Rachel Carey, Laura Delgado, Courtney Taylor, Tatiana Mayfield, Derick Washington and Katrice Reed. Let's continue! I love you.

You can contact the author for speaking engagements or you may purchase her products through:

Jocelyn J. Willis
Sisters with Stories, Inc.
P.O. Box 51013
Fort Worth, TX 76105
Booking:
sisterswithstories@gmail.com

Made in the USA
Monee, IL
14 September 2020